The Little Book of Peace:

101 inspiring ways to add Peace to your work, life, home and dreams

Cherry Menlove

THANKS

❖

My sincere thanks go out to a very small group of people, some of whom I know and some of whom I may never meet, who made writing this book an extraordinary adventure – and one that I will not only never forget but one that I shall continue to grow from.

Those I know – My husband for allowing me to be 'in my head' for almost two months straight and for being so cool with me being thoroughly distracted with this book during the whole of that time.

Aruna Vasudevan (http://www.theliteraryshed.co.uk/) for being the perfect editor for a book of this type. You 'got' everything I was trying to say, even when I was waffling, and you edited it to perfection. I loved our conversations during this time and literally can't wait to do it all again. I hope you feel the same!

Nikki Dupin (http://www.nicandlou.com/) for being the most instinctive and beautiful designer that I have ever come across. You are a very special soul and supremely talented at what you do. Thank you so very much.

Laura Hutchings for proofreading this book in her spare time with moments to spare and for picking up on the very same things of which I was unsure. By doing this, I was able to include exactly what I was meant to include in the book, while still preserving the strength of its message.

Those I do not know – Ludovico Einaudi (http://www. ludovicoeinaudi.com/) for composing the music I listened to almost every day while writing *Peace*. Everything I have ever felt you have managed to put to music and for that I am eternally grateful.

James Altucher (http://www.jamesaltucher.com/) for his book *Choose Yourself*. After I read it, I knew that I could do it on my own. Thank you from the bottom of my heart.

Classic FM (http://www.classicfm.com/) for being in my house daily and for providing an atmosphere of warmth and Peace through both the music that you play and the presenters who have enabled me to heal over the months/years. Music is a tremendously powerful force and this radio station is the most powerful conduit yet.

DEDICATION

❖

This book is dedicated to all the children in the world, including my own. May you come to know Peace deep in your heart early in your lives and may the adults who surround you realize that this knowledge is essential to your well-being, your success and the future of the world in general.

Our twins, Ned & Anaïs. Cannes, France, 2015

INTRODUCTION

❖

I f you ask people what they'd most like to be, disregarding those who immediately shout out 'rich' and/or 'famous', the answer will be 'happy'. And that's a great ambition, don't get me wrong – but it's not enough. Happiness is not enough to sustain us for very long. It is a transitory emotion. It's the feeling that's equivalent to eating something that you've been lusting after for ages. The anticipation and build-up are immense and the experience is initially wonderful. And yet, when you're finished, while you have the memory of something lovely, it fades and things invariably go back to normal. Happiness can last longer than a meal, of course. Happiness can last for weeks, months, even several years – but there's still that light bulb moment when we wake up and we realize that we're not as happy as we once were. And we don't know why. Sometimes, if the unhappiness lasts, we end up making huge life changes in order to get those feelings of happiness back – getting a new job, finding a new partner, moving to a new location, having another baby. And these things may work or they may not. I'm not here to destroy your conception of happiness as I think it's vitally important. What I feel though is that I must share with you something that's an even greater gift than happiness. It is longer lasting, its foundations are stronger, it can weather any storm and it'll give you a sense of confidence that will enable you to manifest your dreams, goals and desires. What is it? It's Peace.

We need Peace in our bodies, hearts, minds, souls and spirits. We need a sense of Peace and a knowledge of Peace to be running through our veins alongside every drop of blood. We need it to be beating our hearts and ruling our thoughts. We need it to be propelling our limbs and working our hands. We need it to be riding the wave of our smiles and carrying the sound of our laughter.

Peace isn't given the credit or attention it deserves. For the most part, it has been consigned to a sign we make with two of our fingers and the joyous carols that we sing at Christmas, instead of being The Force that has the power to change us – and also to change the lives of those around us for the better.

People hanker and chase after love, acceptance, financial freedom, confidence, power, the ability not to be noticed and just blend in and even a quiet life. What they are really searching for is a sense of Peace *within* those situations. Yet, still, the path to Peace remains the road less travelled and that in itself is quite baffling when you discover for yourselves how miraculous a life lived within Peace can be.

I've felt for a long time that our perception of the world and the life we live as humans is not as it should be. I firmly believe that we are meant to live our lives in Peace, abundance and joy. And if you can somehow grasp how important Peace is to your time here on planet earth, you will see your life, both internally and externally, change and shift in ways that you never thought possible. Especially when more challenging times arise.

It's precisely as a result of those times in my life, experienced over a roughly four-year period that Peace came to me. It came during a time of extreme fear, pain, devastation, loss and financial hardship. When I thought I would lose, and did, indeed, lose, almost everything, including, for a time, myself. And yet, out of that period of darkness came my first true experiences of Peace, a state so precious and so life changing that I strive to keep and attain it every moment of every day now.

In this book, you'll find that some of the chapters focus on very practical things that you can do to have, bring and keep Peace into your life. Others still are more conceptual and thought-based. But whichever path you choose to take through this book – whether you read it straight through from cover to cover or simply dip in and out of it, reading a chapter at a time, I want you to be filled with the knowledge that Peace is here, right now, waiting. Whatever your circumstances, it is yours. Take each short chapter and apply it to your life as you see fit and keep in mind that this book is just the beginning. It's the beginning of your lifelong journey to a Peace-full life and a life that will get better and better the further down this road you travel.

My wish for any person reading *The Little Book of Peace* is for them to use it as a way to release more Peace within their own life. And if just one person is able to do that through reading the following chapters, the journey I went on when writing it will be more than worth it. Believe that Peace is out there, waiting for you to grasp hold of it. Believe that you may have Peace in your life, every day, for the rest of your life.

Much love, Cherry Menlove, West Sussex, England, 2015

1 - KNOW IT

❖

There's a decision you have to make right now. I realize that some of you don't like to be told to make decisions. I get that. I won't be told what to do either. But I implore you to make this decision with regards to having Peace in your life. Decide right now that you will, if it's the last thing you ever do, *know* Peace. *Know it?* Yes, *know* it.

Let me go back a bit… In 2011, I first saw a sign that simply said 'Know it' on a shelf in Oprah Winfrey's office in a 'behind the scenes' episode of her show and it jumped out of the TV at me. *Know it?* Know *what?* What does that even mean? At the time, I didn't know what it meant specifically to me and how it would relate to my life and yet I recognized that it was important, vital even, and I knew that it was something I had to remember. I was right and I pass that knowledge on to you now.

This is what you have to 'know' when you are starting a new journey. You have to decide to know that you will succeed. Every single thing that has ever been built, created and achieved (whether for good or bad) has been done with a conscious or subconscious sense of knowing that it will be successful. It's my experience and belief that if you have a conscious sense of knowing where or what you want to go/be/do/have then it will manifest in your life a great deal faster, but manifest it will and there's no stopping it.

So, right now, as you start on this journey of discovery, one of the most important things you can do is to decide that you are going to succeed in finding Peace. Accept this as a fact for your life and a gift that you're going to give to yourself. Peace is an inside job. It is not based on your circumstances (as then it would be happiness), so dig your heels in and believe that however much you've been beaten up by life, however deep in the gutter you find yourself, however high as a kite on adrenaline and nerves you spend your time, you *will* find Peace. The older you get, the more you realize that everything you have ever wanted or dreamed of is already inside you. If it weren't already there, it would be impossible for us to dream it or even think it, as we simply wouldn't recognize it.

So often we wait for others to 'discover us' and we expect

them to do what we have been capable of doing all along, but fear has somehow held us back. Relying on someone else to release or discover something that already lies within you is one of the best examples of giving our power and, therefore, our Peace, away to someone else. That someone else may not respect it or treat what you have given them with the care it deserves, which can then leave us feeling betrayed and unlikely to trust others or ourselves as fully as we might have done. So, if you are starting out on a journey to find more Peace in your life decide here and now that you *will* know Peace in your life. Know it like it is a forgone conclusion. Decide to know it like you've known it all your life. Know it like you've never known anything else. *KNOW IT*. Live it. Breathe it. Speak it. Feel it. Practice it. *Practice* being the operative word. And Peace will be yours.

2 - EVERY BREATH YOU TAKE

❖

What most of us don't know is that Peace is available to us in every moment of the day through the breaths that we take. To stop, if only for a moment, and focus on our breath is one of the most powerful and effective paths to Peace that we can choose to take.

When you feel tension, panic, fear or anger begin to rise in your chest teach yourself to stop for long enough to inhale and exhale, fairly slowly, just once. Stop everything you are doing and breathe in fully, deeply and slowly through your nose. Then exhale, discretely if necessary depending on where you are, through your mouth. Don't make a fuss about doing it and don't put on a show. Just breathe.

You'll notice that the situation you find yourself in slows down, that your mind is clearer and that you are thinking with more clarity and wisdom. You'll notice that anger and frustration lessens and subsides like a balloon with a tiny hole in it, slowly perhaps, but very, very surely. This is a wonderful tool to have in your arsenal. And it works in everything, from someone cutting in the line at Starbucks to a person screaming at you from across the office. You are giving yourself just a second, a heartbeat, a breath to change the direction that this situation is going in.

If you're raising children, it's miraculous, in fact! You'll find Peace within those breaths and the more you practice this, the more Peace you'll have and the less damage you'll do to those tiny people that you love more than anything else in the world. As a mother to twins, I have found myself on the wrong end of frustration more times than I'd like to count. And the feelings of remorse and regret at the things I wish I hadn't said as I watched that spilt glass of juice slowly seeping into the rug, staining it FOREVER, are many. There is always a better way to deal with times of stress than the explosion method. As research has shown, those times, when we think we deserve to vent our spleen, rarely, if ever, make us feel at all better. But they do, inevitably, make us feel *worse*. So, if they make *us* feel worse, how on earth are they going to translate to a five-year old – or, indeed, to anyone we love dearly or have to work with daily?

There absolutely will be times when you loose your cool and this book is not entitled *The Little Book of Becoming Perfect*. It's about Peace, about finding a way to respond to life in a way that brings us the most Peace. As all life begins and ends on our breath, we can unlock and release the tremendous power of Peace in that, too.

You've heard people tell stories about how an accident, incident or tragedy was 'over in a heartbeat'. Well, how about we flip that on its head? How about we realize that we can also turn situations around to our own benefit in a heartbeat by using the power of taking a considered breath, by giving ourselves the priceless gift of taking a moment to think before we act or react.

If you start to follow this practice, then I urge you to keep track of how it evolves and changes you, because it will. You'll be staggered by how such a seemingly teeny, tiny thing can have such a marked effect on your entire life. Write notes, however short, on certain exchanges that were instantaneously diffused by *you* taking a breath and, therefore, choosing a different reaction and path. Watch as you find yourself in these sorts of situations less and less often. Beam with pride as you discover the ability to laugh off things that previously enraged you just a few short weeks ago.

Remember, you're not just 'taking a moment' by doing this, you're dismantling your ego, and scholars and sages alike have been encouraging us to do that for millennia. It won't happen overnight, but it will happen one breath at a time. And, you'll see quite clearly that Peace is readily available to you literally in a heartbeat.

3 - FIND SOMETHING YOU BELIEVE IN

❖

Human beings need something other than themselves to believe in. As John Donne said, 'no man is an island'. Even the most reclusive of us, even if we don't see other people for weeks at a time, draw on something – a certain piece of music that we love or a cat we dote on, for example. We believe in the music we listen to because of the way it makes us feel, just as we believe in the love we have for that cat when it settles down next to us.

We do better in our lives when we have a cause to be passionate about and a reason to get out of bed in the morning. Having a belief in something – anything, at all – helps us to be the very best (or the very worst) version of ourselves. Belief prevents our minds/bodies from atrophying. Believing in something or someone makes it impossible for our hearts, minds and lives to stand still. Because once activated, belief itself takes on motion. And as we hold on to belief, we are, therefore, moving as well.

Find something to believe in, but please choose carefully. We can very easily be led astray by our belief in things outside of ourselves – we see examples of this in extremism of any kind. And so often we can find ourselves believing in someone who, or something that, makes us feel, however subtly, insecure about ourselves. Therefore, try to believe in things that, or people who, enable feelings of Peace. Don't believe in that someone or something because you think that s/he or it will rescue you – that never works. Instead, do so because s/he or it will empower you, will set you free, will inspire you to soar.

I feel incredibly fortunate to be living in an age where so much inspiration and teaching is out there. And, one of the ways we can tell if a teaching or belief is good or right for us is by how it makes us feel. No belief is meant to make us feel drained, confused or powerless. It may challenge us, but it'll be a positive challenge that will make us rise up to meet it with joy and enthusiasm. When we take our thoughts off ourselves and just for a moment think about something other than our hardships, it's remarkable – we feel better. When we feel better, we act better. When we act better, our lives become better. And not better in that fleeting, 'ego-based' way. We feel full and satisfied in a nourished and vibrant way.

Over the next days be open to hearing something that piques your interest. Someone may mention the name of a book or rave about a fantastic yoga teacher s/he has discovered. Being open to anything and afraid of nothing is a prerequisite to living the life we have dreamed of, a life that has Peace at its core. Your strength will be built upon it and you will go on to inspire others. So, trust your feelings, find out as much as you can about the person or topic that interests you. Then watch as the power of believing in something/someone outside of yourself propels you forwards into action, thus enabling more Peace to *flood* into your life.

4 - ONE DAY,
ONE THOUGHT

❖

At the start of this journey to having a more 'Peace-full' life, I believe it's absolutely imperative that you be gentle with yourself. Being gentle with yourself may be an act that you're unfamiliar with and this chapter should help you understand the importance of that concept.

I've often heard it said — and whole-heartedly believe — that if you start the day with a 'To Do' list as long as your arm, then three things will happen:

1. **You'll never get through the list.** It will be a self-perpetuating list, a magic porridge pot of a list that keeps producing more things for you to do.

2. **You'll feel like you've failed.** At the end of each and every day, you'll feel this ever so slightly because you didn't make it to the end of that damned list. You didn't finish the job, No matter that the job was a list of 20 tasks that even a robot would

have had trouble finishing.

3. **You'll feel encumbered/consumed by a sense of failure.** To add insult to injury, at the start of the next day, you'll be encumbered not only by the list you didn't finish yesterday, but also by the new items that you need to add to it today. You'll be consumed by the whole cycle of this slowly, but surely mounting sense of failure.

I'm perhaps being somewhat dramatic, but I want to make the point that we give ourselves too much to do and inevitably end up falling incredibly short of what we would be able to achieve, should we just manage the process better. It's the same with Peace. Make no mistake, living a life that's more Peace-full is going to take practice (although the dividends this effort will pay are unimaginably beneficial) and so we need a route, a road, that we can travel along one step at a time that will ensure we arrive at our Peace-full destination intact, ready to live the lives we know deep inside of us that we are capable of and deserve just by virtue of the fact that we are human beings.

I suggest you start in this way on the road to Peace – using the technique of: **One day, One Thought**. Each morning, wake up and decide on your thought for the day. While you may wish to think of that day's thought upon awakening, personally I wouldn't recommend it. Instead, take some time to sit down and write out **100 *Life Thoughts for the Day*** that are right for you and your life. Then choose from that list on a daily basis. By doing this, you can choose the right thought for what you feel you need most at any particular time in your life. So what sort of thoughts am I referring to? Here are a few from my list:

- I can do it.
- I'm a good mummy.
- I love you, Cherry.
- I'm afraid of nothing.
- Fortune favours the brave.
- If I'm not to live in joy, what am I here for?
- Love or fear?
- If I can see it in my mind, I can see it in my life.
- Something wonderful this way comes.
- Know it.
- Kindness is strength.
- There is nobody else like me.
- There is no lack of ANYTHING in my life.

Do you get the picture? These are simple thoughts that I've needed to have on repeat in my head at certain times in my life. I've chosen the thought that is most applicable to me, the moment I wake up and if my mind begins to wander into no-man's land by the time I'm up and making coffee, then I simply repeat my chosen thought in my head like a mantra. It brings me right back to the truth in the situation and stops me from going crazy. By doing this, you're also training your brain. You won't need to use this technique forever because at some point your mind will become so adept at choosing the right thought the first time around that you won't need to refer to your list at all. However, when you're starting out on your journey into Peace, working on the basis of One Day, One Thought helps. It speeds up the process of Peace exponentially, is deceptively simplistic and yet so powerful.

5 - THE PEACE IN NATURE & THE NATURE OF PEACE

❖

It's astonishing to me that I have waited so long to truly absorb the fact that Nature is absolutely vital to my health, well-being and joy. Living, studying and working for most of my adult life in predominantly urban areas, I stopped coming into contact with open space, Nature or its glory. And glorious, it most certainly is. City life often makes you feel like you'll be missing something vital if you're not there to witness or experience it. So we keep to the city confines and then wonder why we don't feel better than we do because we're being suffocated. The countryside scares some people, without a doubt. They're not used to the scary open space and the decidedly different pace of life, which seems a lot slower and can send certain people into a bit of a panic. And yet Nature, in her power and elegance, does two things simultaneously, if we let her: she forces us to gently question ourselves, and what we believe; and she holds us in the palm of her hand while we do so. It's up to us if we trust her methods, but I assure you that it's what she does best. She is our inspiration and our protector, but you have to be able to witness her in all her glory to experience this. I don't believe that you have to look far to truly know the power that Nature can have in your life. Some examples include:

- **Witnessing lambs jump in the air.** I'm not kidding, it's one of the most powerful and joy inducing sights you will ever see.
- **Seeing huge swathes of flowers in season.** Great examples of this are bluebells in woods, cow parsley in hedgerows, roses in the garden. Of course, I'm in England so these species are applicable to the country I live in, but each and every country has its own examples.
- **An open sky.** Uninterrupted by any buildings of any kind.
- **The smell of the outdoors on an early autumn morning.** By this, I mean the smell of the air as it changes from season to season. This is almost imperceptible, but it changes us. To witness the changing of the seasons brings hope and confidence in the future as we see that time is constantly on the move and nothing stays the same forever.

Nature goes on without us and I've found that it's far better for us to follow Nature and live according to her schedule than to ignore it completely. Or, even worse, try to alter the natural course of things when it comes to living on planet earth. This brings me to the second point about Nature. After it has revealed to us its magnificence, its confidence, its creativity and basically shown us up in virtually every way possible, it then gives us the most amazing gift we could ask for. It protects us as we dare to go inwards to heal and grow.

There is Peace in Nature and Nature's Peace-full nature is there to serve us, enhance our experience and offer us the world. I had the most startling example of this one time when I was Yosemite National Park in California. It felt, at the time, as if everything I knew to be true was disappearing and my life as I knew it was changing dramatically. I was walking through the park and turned a corner to be faced with the famous view of Half Dome, the granite monolith that rises out of the earth and stands at almost 5,000 ft above the forest floor. I knew in an instant as I stared up that if that rock, which had been there for upwards of 66 million years, could cope with all that had been thrown at it, I would get through my current chapter. I felt as if my surroundings were taking care of me, holding me, allowing me just to float through this time in numbness and offering to take the slack. *THAT* is the power of Nature and although the example I've given is fairly extreme, albeit one that was needed during a period of great loss, if I have Nature present in my life on a daily basis, I have not only a constant source of inspiration for my work, but also a sense of protection, wonder and Peace as I travel through life.

6 - RELAX INTO PEACE

---- ❖ ----

When I discover something that I love or want more of, I seem to make a concerted effort to get more of it – *'effort'* being the operative word. Effort is the very antithesis of Peace: the two cannot co-exist together. And if you make an effort to get more of it in your life it will run away, like rainwater through your hands. We must relax into Peace, which, if you think about it, should sound like a huge relief. I mean how often are we told that in order to attain something we want or desire we must relax into it? Not that often. We're encouraged to work ourselves into exhaustion because that's what makes a winner, apparently. We're told to sweat blood, beat the competition, work the longest hours, have the biggest following and make the most money.

Winning a contract, customers, a role or a job is something to be celebrated and felt deeply as an achievement and joy. But it is different from being in constant competition with everyone you meet and seeing them as an enemy that needs to be slayed. Effort carries a certain type of energy; a sense of competition carries a certain type of energy. Being competitive carries the same. And although it won't be immediately apparent, the energy these types of behaviours carry are not that good for us. And over time we'll pay the price for it by having to deal with the symptoms of stress. Relaxation also carries energy. A positive energy that translates into a mindset, which then morphs into a thought and turns into behaviour which can influence the way our life goes. With some energies you'll gain Peace – and with others, you most certainly will not. Using a positive energy to gain Peace is one of the most effective ways I know to change a situation from effort to Peace. It has an awful lot to do with letting go and an awful lot to with choice, both of which are in our hands and under our control. And combined they make relaxation. Which enables us to walk through the doors of Peace with our arms and our hearts open so wide that we'll be consumed by what greets us.

7 - WHAT DO YOU HAVE ALREADY?

---- ❖ ----

It's very easy for us as humans to miss the Peace that gratitude gives us when we are thankful for what we already have in our lives. Yet, if we don't know gratitude, we are unconscious. And to be unconscious is to be alive, but not living. And, to me that's a pretty scary place to be.

A great many of us will have seen people with huge material wealth bemoaning something that isn't quite right. A detail they believe has been forgotten, a moment that wasn't as perfect as they'd paid for it to be, a gift that they didn't ask for and didn't want. We refer to these as 'first-world problems' and it's extraordinarily easy to be offended by such vacuous behavior. But a lack of gratitude spans all of society, from the wealthiest to the poorest.

I worked in Brazil for two months within both the favelas of Rio de Janeiro and Curitiba in southern Brazil. I saw two different sets of people dealing with the extreme poverty there: those who were angry at what they felt they had been given and others, who were, in contrast, so grateful. The first group were unhappy that they had no money, no opportunity, no luck, no support, bad parents, bad housing, a bad god who was angry with them, and so on. Some of the families in that particular favela on the Rio hillside had several generations living with them. Raw sewage ran down the hill in front of the houses, there were very few jobs and we were shown up the hill by little boys in dirty shorts carrying loaded handguns. A great many of them were parents with children to support and here I was, a 20-year old bringing food and supplies into their neighbourhood and their turf. I listened to them with the utmost respect, but at the end of the day, I got to leave there and come home to follow my dream of going to drama school. The second group of people I met had a different light shining out of their eyes and they were some of the most generous people I have ever experienced being with. They had nothing materially, but everything soulfully. They had little themselves, but gave you everything. They didn't believe in lack, but only in abundance so, of course, they gave you what they had, as they knew it would be replaced with better. These people were so grateful for what they had that they managed to be able to give from within it and thus were at Peace with themselves. By behaving in this way, they created a vacuum for *more* to enter their lives. *More* education, *more* money, *more* clothing, *more* understanding, *more* patience. Whatever it was they dreamed of having in the future, in the present, they had decided that they lacked for nothing, that they would wear an attitude of gratitude and move forwards in strength, joy and, therefore, Peace.

I've never forgotten the attitude of members of that community and now when I get set upon by feelings of dissatisfaction, I immediately focus my thoughts on what I already have. By the time I've listed the third or fourth thing, I'm already feeling suitably embarrassed for even thinking about moaning and there's power in dismantling the ego in such a way.

Please don't ever fall into the trap of believing that being ungrateful or dissatisfied keeps you on the cutting edge of your destiny. It doesn't. In fact, it keeps it from your door. Your life will be so full of complaint that there will be no room for anything else, certainly no satisfaction when it comes. So, if you're new to this practice, start with right where you're sitting and give thanks. It can be as simple as giving thanks for the hands that are holding your digital device right now or the eyes that can read the words. There, you've done it. You've started on yet another path to Peace. That of gratitude and thankfulness. There's no stopping the miracles that are coming your way now.

8 - ADVENTURES IN FAILING

❖

Failure, or the feelings and perception of failure, can be crippling and certainly don't bring Peace. They can both embarrass us when we recall how stupid we feel we've been in the past and they can also stop us in our tracks from attempting to do anything of the same ilk ever again. We hear daily how one person *failed* at business while another *failed* at their marriage. A couple has *failed* to have children and another *failed* at parenting the ones they were lucky enough to be given. A footballer *failed* to score a goal and an actress *failed* to win a role. Judgement from others is rife both online and in the press, as well as at the school gate and around the water cooler: nobody is really safe from it.

But know this; there are very, very few situations in life that cannot be rescued, rectified, revived and resuscitated and it drives me nuts when most of these situations are referred to as failures (and then bring on with them the unwarranted feelings that come with such apparent failure). What they actually are is *adventures*.

Let's take the person in business. People rarely venture into the business world with a blueprint of success. Many successful people have huge learning curves to master before hitting the jackpot and many of their businesses *'fail'*. But if you talk to any one of those people who've succeeded, you will never hear them refer to their journey as a 'series of failures'. How can you possibly think of yourself as a failure and still succeed? It's not something that can be done. But you can be a 'Person of Adventure' and rise to great heights. You can be a person with some crazy stories to tell and still be sitting there in the place that you knew you'd get to no matter what challenges you have had to deal with.

As people we're all so fallible and the word 'fail' is such a misnomer for what is actually the giant tapestry that makes up every single one of our lives. Here's how the feeling of failure manifests itself within us, as:

- Sadness
- Tiredness
- Fear
- The unwillingness to ever try something again

- Tension
- Stress
- Headaches
- Anger
- Guilt
- Rage
- Addiction
- Insecurity
- Arrogance
- Sexual dysfunction
- Panic attacks
- Depression

You get the picture. Here's how the feeling of having had the adventure of a lifetime manifests and feels no matter what the outcome, as:

- Bravery
- Exhilaration
- Achievement
- Love
- Courage
- Happiness
- Joy

- Experience
- Confidence
- Hope
- Certainty
- Creativity
- Energy
- Humour
- Lightheartedness
- Success
- Friendship
- Good memories

Failing – or the perception of it (I don't believe we ever fail if we try) – needs rebranding. It needs Don Draper to go in and 'smooth' it over. We need to be encouraged to get off our arses and throw our hat into the ring and know right at the start that we will be standing there at the end of it and be able to say '*I TRIED. And I'll continue to try until my last day here on earth. And you know why? Because that is what LIFE is. Moments in time that I intend to fill with adventure. Failure? I know not of that concept or even that word*'

That level of trust in yourself and in a universe that adores you will bring you Peace. I promise.

9 - GUILT-FREE = PEACE-FULL

❖

'I felt really guilty when I said that.'

'I shouldn't have done that, I feel guilty now.'

'I love being a working mum but I feel guilty about it.'

'I feel pretty guilty that I get to be at home with my children all day and I love it.'

'Ugh, she really knows how to really lay it on thick and make me feel guilty!'

'He only has to look at me and I feel guilty, like I've done something wrong.'

Let me tell you something that I realized a very long time ago, but only really learned within the last three years – other people are not thinking about you. It's unfortunate, as we're all really special of course, but they are just not. They are thinking about themselves and any feelings of guilt that other people project on to you are just that –

projections. Making others feel guilty for something is a magnificent way to control. And the ones who use guilt in their arsenal are very good at knowing where to land the punches. Motherhood, fatherhood, parenthood, work ethic, career choice, partner choice are all fantastic subjects that may put your back up when you are probably just about getting over the last attack of feeling guilty about something. It's pernicious and takes away your Peace at a moment's notice.

For those landing the punches however, once they've hit the target, they move on. They have rid themselves of the poison building up inside of them, off-loading it on to you instead – and so while they're now free to go about their day, you are left wondering if you've made the right choice, are lazy, demanding, mistaken or unfeeling, which isn't right. So, take the time to consciously recognize who those people are in your life and decide now to reject the toxicity that they ever so kindly bestow upon you!

You don't have to say anything, do anything or even change the way you talk to them. You simply make up your mind not to allow those 'flippant' comments to penetrate for a moment longer. Does that sound too easy?

Too difficult? Well, yes, it's a choice you make in your own mind. But once you've made it and are quite certain that is the direction that you are now going in, the energy that you employ, which is actually forgiveness surprisingly, takes care of the rest. Without effort, you get to deflect the old feelings of unnecessary guilt that people are trying to drape you in while remaining anger, bitterness and confusion free. Ask yourself one question at the time of attack: 'how does this make me feel?' If it makes you feel anything less than hopeful, empowered, excited or – and this is important – relieved, then reject it. Silently and in Peace, but, still, reject it. Don't confuse the pain of others with the voice of your own life leading you in the right direction. Your life and your heart will gently guide you with nudges that inspire and excite you. They won't make you feel like you're practically worthless.

The world supports you, naturally, using the power and energy of love and it's not about to change the habits of a lifetime. So get centered, stay sweet and make room for the Peace that's about to enter the door to your heart and mind.

10 - FIND YOUR RITUAL

—————— ❖ ——————

There's Peace to be found in rituals. What sort of rituals am I talking about? Rituals that you have created, tailored to fit and formed to your own requirements, over time.

OK, let's talk about my most important personal ritual – coffee. In the morning I have a coffee. And it's the same type of coffee that I have every day (two Nespresso pods, one pink and one black with lacto-free skimmed milk), in a very large mug. I have it upon awakening before I've had breakfast. I look forward to it daily and I wake up earlier than I have to, purely to ensure that it's not rushed. This is all part of my ritual. I sometimes use the time while I'm drinking the coffee to think. Think about my 'Life Thought' for the day, think about the present time in my life and think about the future for a moment or two. I use this ritual to generally get my thinking straight before I launch into the day. Then, at other times, I use the ritual to clear my mind of thoughts, to not think. To start afresh with no expectations of the day to follow. Having this ritual ensures that my day never, ever starts off without me being prepared. I have two young children and a husband who leaves very early for work and returns home late at night so the children are my responsibility during the week. I also work full-time and do the daily school-run to and from school. I volunteer there, helping out in the Drama department and on the PTA. So, like every other person I know, I am busy. Waking up earlier to ensure that I have this time to have coffee and to collect myself is absolutely vital to my well-being in emotional, physical and spiritual terms. I find Peace at the start of the day, which means that I don't have to go searching for it later on.

With the lives that we live today, making a sacrifice in order to protect a personal ritual is absolutely worth it. We've made it this way, this frantic, this connected, this busy. But whether your ritual is one of coffee alone in the morning, a 15-minute meditation during your lunch hour, a slice of cake on the sofa with the dog before school pick-up or 50 minutes pounding the streets of the city in which you live at 11 pm, then I urge you to create it, stick to it and protect it. Why? Because you need it. I promise, you need it for your personal Peace.

11 - WHERE YOU LOOK, YOU FIND

❖

Some things are so obvious that we miss them. It happens. After all, we're bombarded with information daily. Our lives are busy and everything is pretty much automatic and electronic. But when someone else is controlling the content that we see on a day-to-day basis (under the guise of letting us make our own choices), we are often at the mercy of his/her particular agenda. When things are simply presented to us – through news outlets, social media platforms, iPhones, iPads, smart devices or on TV or the radio – we may absorb pictures, words, thoughts, philosophies and actions that are incredibly far removed from where we'd like or want to be, putting us at odds with our own goals and vision for our lives. And that's, of course, going to have an affect on us and impact on our sense of Peace.

This was brought home to me one afternoon, when I was home alone and using my iPhone to look at a social network. I hit the screen in the wrong place while scrolling down and unintentionally pressed 'Play' on a video of a man being tortured. The camera was in close up and although it was only seconds I've never forgotten what I saw. This is an extreme case and something parents the world over worry about when their children are online unsupervised.

There is also the more subversive type of information that gets through the filter of what we should be subjecting ourselves to. This is the type of content that leaves us feeling ever so slightly robbed. By that I mean that we are being robbed of joy, robbed of inspiration and robbed of confidence, robbed of satisfaction at what we already have. And, most of the time, we don't even know it's happening. This is an extremely subtle way of altering our mood and our opinions of things but when we are blithely scrolling through and paying little attention to those feelings building up, over time they can leave us bereft of the very qualities that bring us Peace. I think this is a new behaviour. I know that my parents didn't have access to this amount of content when I was growing up and that we, as children, at the time, certainly didn't. But then that's the subtle perniciousness of it all – we don't know how it's affecting us until we switch it off. Our minds are our hard-drives and it's vital that we only download the highest calibre information onto them.

So, instead of our smart devices, let's look to Nature, to our friends, to our children; let's look to fresh food, to documentaries made by brave people and books written by courageous survivors. Let's choose where we look and what we find. If we choose our content judiciously, we will experience Peace in a rather profound way and our lives will simply be more Peace-full.

12 - LOSS IN OUR LIVES

❖

I'm obsessed with creating vacuums. Once a vacuum has been created, it is an empty space for something else to come in and occupy it. If the vacuum itself has been created with the right intention then what will come in can only be the highest and best for your life. That's simply the law of attraction at work. And it can help to bring Peace/make our lives more Peace-full. 'There is no lack' is a mantra of mine. It particularly fits when I'm busy creating new vacuums. And yet to do this, I have to let things go. And the concept of 'letting go' is a very scary prospect to most people; it certainly was to me, when I first embraced it. So this chapter deals with helping you do so – with shrinking your world to make it bigger through the power of letting things go.

Here's how I started – with losing 'stuff'. We recently moved house. We downsized from a home of around 3,500 sq ft to just over 1,000 sq ft. This meant that I had to lose a lot of 'stuff'. It was just about the most cathartic exercise I have ever experienced. I was ruthless first of all because I knew I had to be, but after a while I started to enjoy it. I had criteria and unless the object met it, it would be donated, recycled or sold. My criteria was a combination of when I used it last, how big it was and how it made me feel when I looked at it. If I didn't use it regularly, if it wasn't going to fit into our cottage Peacefully and if it drained me of energy due to some memory or connection, then it was out the door never to return. Each and every day in the build-up to our move I was creating vacuums. And almost every day since we have moved into our new house, I have continued to create even more.

It's very freeing to only have the very best of your possessions around you at all times. Everything you look at you like and everything you use makes you feel good. I'm also not a believer in storing your 'best' stuff away and only getting it out on special occasions, I have it out and ready to use. Clearing the clutter in our homes is a very simple yet deceptively powerful way to practice the art of letting go (and I still have a way to go with this) because sometimes in life we will be forced to let go of things (be they people, jobs or security of some sort), in an instant. This kind of shock can bring us to our knees, sometimes never to get back up again.

Life will without doubt contain loss, that's a given. But, when a healthy attitude of letting go is nurtured over time without putting fear in us, it can prepare us for anything in life that contains loss of some sort.

This goes back to the very reason why I believe we have challenges in life – to pass on the wisdom and give the pain value. And to enable us to continue on in joy, abundance and Peace. But this can only happen if we are prepared for loss the best way we can be ahead of time, otherwise it blindsides us. Loss doesn't have to be the worst thing that has ever happened to us. It can be the best. And when looking back on it, it can be the bringer of incalculable Peace in to our lives. So begin to see your losses as vacuums for goodness to flood in to, instead of holes that will never be filled.

13 - BE HERE NOW. PEACE IN THE PRESENT.

❖

othing exists for us but this moment. Right now. Ha! That's gone. And now we're on to this moment … right now … right now … Aa–a– and another one! Those past few seconds are now memories. They don't exist now. They're gone. They've been lived, experienced and felt. The moments that are still to come don't exist yet either. They are our dreams; they are our dreads.

We don't experience the past or the future in the same way as we do the present moment. The right now! And, even that's now gone. When you think of time in this way it becomes a stark and rather beautiful reminder of the importance of being 'present'. Of being in the 'now'. There's very little point in remaining within moments that are just memories and even less point in living in moments that haven't even happened yet.

Yes. I can hear what you're saying to me right now… *'But I want to plan for things.'* So plan, but plan in the present.

Think the thoughts, dream the dream, *trust* it and get back to making right now as amazing as you possibly can.

'*But what about visualizing the future?*' You can do that automatically while still being present. We can do more than one thing at a time.

'*I have beautiful memories of the past.*' Then take the strength of them into the present moment with you to inform the now and make it stronger.

'*But things will never be as good as they once were.*' There is no lack.

'*How can you be this certain that staying present will give you such an amazing future?*' Because my own personal prayer is: 'This or something even better, please.'

And, in that very short prayer lies my Peace.

14 - THE COMPETITION MYTH

❖

We live in a competitive world. We compete for everything: jobs, money, friends, followers, success. So let me start this chapter by letting you in on a secret. You're not in competition with anyone else on this planet and you never, ever will be. For one reason: there's only one of you. Think about it just for a moment. There is only:

- One person on this planet who has seen the things that you have seen in the exact way that you have seen them.
- One person in the whole of the world who has those feelings related to what you've seen.
- One human being who has experienced life the exact way you have experienced it.
- One human who does the job the way you do it.
- One woman who gave birth to the child that you gave birth to.
- One man who fathered the child you have had.

- One writer who will write the words you write in that exact order.
- One CEO who has *your* vision for the business.
- One person who will love another in the way that you will love them.

There is no lack:
- Of anything, ever, so there is no competition.
- Of money in the world.
- Of world and life-changing businesses to be set up.
- Of love.

There is no one like you, with your particular dreams, desires, vision and faith for what your life and this world could become. And these don't have to be huge global dreams either. There is nobody on this planet who would run that village store like you, work from that wood yard like you, raise those children like you, tend to that garden like you. No one. Not now. And not ever. Think about the way *you* smile, the way *you* hug, the way *you* reach out, spontaneously, for a person's hand when you know they need holding. There is no lack, and the sooner you live, act and behave from that belief, the sooner you'll see your life overflow with everything good that is right there, waiting for you. Trust that there is enough because there is. Yes, that's simplistic, but it's also true. Yes, for far too long the distribution of certain things has been amoral. But that still doesn't mean that these things don't exist.

From when I was small, I wanted to act. I first stepped on to a set at the age of 11 and, from that day forward, apart from my parents all the grown-ups around me (even the actors in work) repeatedly said that 80 percent of actors are unemployed at any one time! Well, if that mantra is repeated, there's nothing else for it to do but to manifest. That's an entire profession (industry even) that's potentially been (and is being) robbed of some amazingly talented actors who might have torn up the screen and stage if they only they hadn't been fearful; if only they hadn't believed the B.S. about employment percentages. Don't be stolen from. There is no lack. Trust this and you'll feel the Peace physically enter your heart, mind and soul.

15 - LOVE

❖

Love doesn't make the giver or the receiver feel 'less-than'.

Love doesn't strategize.

Love doesn't make things complicated.

Love doesn't believe that Love will ever run out so it keeps giving of itself.

Love doesn't know fear.

Love is so secure in itself it can sometimes make people feel nervous.

Love knows that this is OK because love doesn't know what an ego is.

Love doesn't care. Because it's love.

Love is so magnificently powerful that it can be scary. So sometimes people would rather feel fear, doubt and pain instead.

Love keeps you here when you want to go somewhere, *ANYWHERE*, else.

Love wakes you up when you want to sleep and sleep and sleep.

Love enables forgiveness in the midst of hatred. Which isn't really hatred at all but just fear.

Fear is no match for love.

Peace is a natural access point for love and when everything that isn't love is recognized only as fear then that fear will disappear because nothing survives in the face of love. Nothing has to, it's totally and utterly complete.

16 - SIMPLE EXCITEMENT

❖

When was the last time you felt excitement? I realized a few years ago that, along with a sense of Peace, excitement in my life seemed to diminish with age. This was astonishing to me: This was my life, the only one in this form that I would ever experience, so why was I not excited by it? How could I have let this happen? I think it's as simple as having just got used to the situation and becoming a bit cynical after not knowing how to deal with the knocks that life had thrown at me. I'd lost my Peace, while at the same time I'd reached a plateau of sorts. Some may call this state being jaded; others may call it maturity. Some may call it cynicism; others may call it being a realist. Whatever the label, I'd lost something really quite precious – excitement. And now I knew it was gone, I missed it. I missed that quiver that would go down my shoulders and into my tummy – the anticipation that something was about to happen. The quiver that came at different ages and stages right through my life when I thought of Santa, the school holidays, going on a date, securing a job, travelling, reading a good book, getting married, having babies, moving house etc.

Although I'd achieved so much in my life by this point, I didn't quite know where to turn to regain that zest and enthusiasm for something wonderful. Don't misunderstand me, my family give and have given me great joy, that's without doubt, but there was a sense of personal excitement that I felt was missing and wanted to retrieve for myself. So I began to dismantle what excitement had meant to me previously and rebuild it. Life is cyclical at all times and, instead of panicking, I readjusted my course, re-set what excitement meant to me and made a decision to open my eyes to new things that would and could excite me now. It has been quite an experience opening oneself up to anything and I've been surprised by the diversity of things that add excitement to my life now.

One of the defining characteristics is that these things are very, very simple. So here are just a few of the simple things that excite me today:

- The first sip of coffee in the morning.
- Going on holiday with my husband and children.
- Autumn.

- My husband coming in from work in the evening.
- The smell of cinnamon, in any form but particularly on Christmas Eve, in my kitchen.
- Our pub lunch as a family on Christmas Eve before going home to 'hunker down'.
- New BBC dramas.
- Seeing a deer on a dog walk.
- The first shoots of green after a long winter.

I told you they were simple! Of course this doesn't mean that my life has now become deathly dull and a series of moments waiting for coffee and deer spotting. Life is wonderful and I put a large part of being able to actually recognize that down to re-setting my points of excitement. Simple things ground me. They make me stop and look and create and wonder and *LIVE* them instead of rush through them. It's wonderful. Try it, please try it. It's not dull, it's exciting. And, more to the point, it's Peacefull.

17 - YOUR OWN PEACE-FULL PLACE

❖

I have been writing about home and our home lives since 2006, when I started my first blog. It seemed natural to me: although I dearly love to travel and have adventures, there's something extremely valuable about having a home that works for me. It isn't about the house, the size or the facilities, but about the feeling and the atmosphere within it. It's about whether or not the house serves me or whether I serve the house.

When my husband was in hospital, having treatment for cancer to which he wasn't responding, it was a very, very scary time. I awoke confused from a deep sleep one morning, and I could hear the twins, who had just turned one, gurgling away for their breakfast. I looked over to where Robert should have been, had always been up until that point, and suddenly remembered what was happening. He wasn't there. He might not be there again. What was I going to do? From the time it took me to get myself out of bed, walk down the hall, and enter the bedroom where my children were blissfully unaware of anything other than the fact that they were hungry, I decided that I would make our lives work. I decided that my children would be raised in a home of love and security, joy and Peace. It was that which gave me the strength to go into them that morning with a smile on my face and greet them with a 'good morning', instead of bursting into tears as soon as I saw them. And I put that strength largely down to the fact that I felt the house we were in at that time was our home. I felt safe there and I knew it would hold me up and protect me at this time. It would allow for Peace and relaxation, laughter and fun. Pottering and creativity.

That's my story, but I urge you to find that place for yourselves. It's vital. Throw out all misconceptions about what 'home' *should* be like or what you've experienced in the past and seek the place that's truly *yours*, no matter how long it takes. Peace awaits you there. Deep, deep Peace.

18 - NO MORE DRAMA

We all know people who thrive on a little bit of drama. Whether it's a gossipy tidbit or a full-blown catastrophe, there is something about drama that makes us feel alive. But if there's one thing I know with absolute certainty now it's that drama, and the encouragement of it in our lives, is very, very bad for us. How do I know this? Well, many years ago I used to love a bit of drama. It validated me and made me feel like I had something to say and something to contribute. It was an adrenaline rush of emotions that never satisfied me. What was I looking for that made me seek it in drama? What was I missing that made dramatic moments in my life seem worthwhile? Confidence, emotional intelligence, sensitivity, wisdom? Possibly. I was certainly missing Peace in my life, I know that.

When Peace is missing, we can occasionally go in the opposite direction and stir things up, thinking that if we ruffle a few feathers or unsettle the waters, we'll somehow *feel* what we so desperately miss. But, of course, it's simply not going to come through those means and we have to trust in the process of having Peace in our life instead of drama. Trust in Peace itself. Peace is more than a feeling, Peace is energy and it's extremely strong. When you are at Peace within yourself, you become like a moth to a flame to other people, while at the same time being able to remain utterly calm and wise in the presence of what you'll recognize as THEIR drama. When you are at Peace, you'll be able to offer advice (if asked for it) and invariably sit back and watch as folk do the exact opposite to what you've suggested as their drama is addictive to them. And it can be tough to give that up, like any addiction really.

Is it plain sailing on the other side of drama? No, not at all. Some of the most dramatic times of my life happened long after I'd given drama up. You see, when you chase drama you're distracted from chasing your *true* calling in life and that is where your heart and soul lies. That is where the excitement sits, not in some incident that doesn't even involve you or an event that you orchestrate to keep you the focus of everybody's attention (constant ailments is a good one, watch out for those.) You'll still have challenges to face because that's life but they will happen for one reason and one reason only: in order for us to squeeze the wisdom out of them over time, pass that on to others and then move forwards ourselves in joy and abundance. That is what changes the world. That is what brings Peace on earth. And that is what we're here for. That is love incarnate and it has absolutely nothing to do with drama. Nothing at all.

19 - PEACE MIRRORS PEACE

❖

Peace mirrors Peace back at you.

Choose to think Peace-full thoughts and a mind full of Peace will be yours.

Choose to act Peacefully, no matter what the provocation and a Peace-full life will be yours.

Choose to consume food and drink that brings Peace to your body, mind and soul and your body will serve you by working for you in Peace.

Choose to speak Peace-full words and your experience will be one of seeing Peace on earth.

Spend your money in ways that add Peace and don't detract from it. Be Peace-full and Peace will be returned to you.

Simple.

Powerful.

True.

20 - GO GENTLY

❖

When the word 'gentle' is mentioned in conversation, it usually conjures up rather saturated images of people holding babies or kittens frolicking about on freshly laundered bedding. And yet, being gentle, first with ourselves, and then with others, is an extremely smart way to go about your day. Being gentle with ourselves means having absolutely no harsh words or thoughts to or about ourselves when things don't immediately go to plan. That is: No utterances of 'you idiot' under our breaths when we make a mistake and our boss finds out. No confessions of being 'a bad mother' when we refuse our children a second ice cream and they have a public fit. No anxious waking in the middle of the night when we recall something that we genuinely have forgotten because our plates were stacked so high with all we have to do on a daily basis. *That's* being gentle with ourselves. And what the heck happened to that? With telling ourselves that it's actually OK. That no human being would have remembered that tiny detail. And that the world is not, repeat, **NOT** going to end because we forgot something.

The way we speak to ourselves, within the confines of our own thoughts, is extraordinary and we often end up being our own worst enemy. If a stranger were to hear us they'd accuse us of verbal assault. And yet we do it. We do it to the most precious of people: ourselves. No one can be as hard on us as we are on ourselves but, in a world where criticism from others is a foregone conclusion, it's really important that we learn to treat ourselves gently and with respect. It may take you a while to get used to thinking of yourself as the most precious person there is (and that isn't what this particular chapter is about), but let me quickly add that you are not going to be able to reach your full potential in any field until you put that correct value on yourself. Not an inflated ego-based value. And not a dis-ingenuous humble value either, but the right one. The one that marks you out simply as a human being and that's a good place to start.

Choose to be gentler when carrying out tasks. Move more gently. There's no need to rush everywhere. Speak more gently with others and slow your thoughts down just a lit-tle bit. It gives you time to think more gently, react more gently and puts the possibility of those kneejerk reactions occurring on the backburner for a time (you can always whip one out later, if need be). To slow down, take care of, tend to, nurture and encourage is something that is very far from weak and passive. It's a conscious move into strength and brings with it a sense of Peace that is rooted in confidence ... with not a frolicking puppy in sight.

21 - LAZY

❖

Doing nothing is not what I would call laziness. Sometimes it's vital that we do nothing or we'll burn out. *Being* nothing is certainly what I would call laziness. In fact, I'd go a step further and call it stealing. By not 'being' the person you were meant to be you are robbing the rest of us of *you*. Unique, precious, wonderful you.

Be love.
Be kindness.
Be wisdom.
Be generosity.
Be entrepreneurial.
Be a ball-breaker.
Be a lone voice.
Be Peace-full.
Just BE!

22 - STOP RIGHT NOW

❖

Stop right now! No matter what you're doing, *stop!* Now look around and list 10 things that you're thankful for. I'll do it to show you what I mean. I am thankful for:

1. The hot cup of tea I've just made.
2. The music playing on the radio.
3. My computer working.
4. The rain starting to clear.
5. The encouraging email I just got.
6. The apple tree that fell down that is no longer a danger.
7. Christmas only being three months away.
8. The fact that I'm here, right now, at this time in history.
9. My children being healthy.
10. My husband being healthy.

It may not look like much, but that list is actually pretty powerful. It means I'm present. That I'm here in the moment, that I've an attitude of gratitude and I'm not anxious but at Peace. I can achieve anything from that starting point.

23 - PASSION AND COURAGE

❖

Passion and courage. Ugh, if only we could just have the passion. Live our passion, see our passion, feel and experience the outcome of our passions. Forget needing courage. I'm not courageous, we say. I don't want to be courageous, that's too risky. It's hard enough just being passionate for goodness' sake! But the brutal truth is we need both, I'm afraid. And although I hate it as much as you do, passion and courage are inseparable.

What I didn't realize for long time was that passions are grown and developed *within* our courage. They come alive and flourish when we're courageous with them because at that moment we give them something that absolutely no one else can – our true selves. They fully become our passions when they contain a piece of us – and that can only be channelled through courage.

So, that's the bad news but keep on reading before you rip up that business plan or choose another path because there's something that doesn't get said often enough. Just because you have to be brave doesn't mean that seeing your dreams and visions come true is going to be about having a lifelong struggle with courage. Quite the opposite, in fact. When you are following the right passion for you the courage required appears naturally. You won't be left floundering without it, but you do have to keep your eyes open to recognize it when it comes.

Most of us travel down a road of experimentation and exploration before we find our feet in life and courage will often be required to do that. But you know that you're on the right track in life when that courage stops becoming forced and starts to flow very naturally. It starts to excite you a little bit and you begin to look at yourself and see a side to yourself that you probably never knew existed. That is when passion and courage collide in perfect unison. And although you may be in, what appears to be, the eye of a storm there's Peace there. And by god you'll know it.

24 - THE PEACE FOUND IN RELIEF

❖

A great many things that are worth doing take time, concentration and use up our natural resources. There is no getting away from that sometimes. We have projects, life experiences, goals and dreams that are bloody painful to see through to completion on occasion – and even when they are over, no matter how much we've put in and however successful they have been, sometimes it doesn't feel like all that effort has been worth it. And then there are those situations that, after a little or a lot of contemplation, we pull the plug on and we immediately feel better.

Shall I tell you how you know whether you've made the right decision? Relief. If you feel a sense of relief, then you have almost certainly made the right choice. There is immense Peace in relief.

Relief is something that I don't think we focus on as much as we should because in my opinion it's up there with excitement, fun, a sense of well-being and wholeness. When you KNOW that you've made the right decision (by the sense of relief you feel) you are, in that time and place, taking 100 percent responsibility for the WHOLENESS and largesse of your life. And, you know when you're doing *that* because you feel empowered – more energetic, more inspired, less self-conscious and you have more core-confidence. That's not to say that there won't be times when making those choices isn't hard. They can be some of the hardest decisions we ever make and the effects can be far reaching. But when you feel relief wash over you, no matter how well hidden or buried it is, you can rest assured in the knowledge that there is something incredibly and powerfully authentic in your choice. It's **you** being **you**, the best **you**, the true **you**, the benevolent **you** in all your glory. And there is *NOTHING* better than a human being operating in all his or her glory. I've seen it a number of times and it is one of the most inspiring and joyful things you'll ever see.

Relief is a resting place of total safety and security, even when you might not have realized that you needed one. But allow me to let you in on a secret. Your body knew, your spirit knew, your soul knew, even when your conscious mind was still business as usual.

If you are currently in the middle of making a decision that you're struggling with then spend some time and ask yourself whether you would feel relief if you made a choice one way or the other. Be prepared, in some cases, for there to be some kind of fall out, occasionally there is, but I've found that the relief gives you a certain strength to cope with that.

Towards the start of this year, way back when it was really cold and dank, Robert and I took the children to the movies. As we walked down the street of the busy town centre afterwards, I looked in the window of an estate agent. It was an involuntary act – Robert and I hadn't been thinking about moving house (again). But the house I saw in that window was a small cottage – square and neat in its shape; cosy and small in its size. We had decided to move house by the end of that day. There was TREMENDOUS relief in the air the few days following that moment and we hadn't even been discussing a move. We didn't need, or even want, to live elsewhere. But shall I tell you how we both knew it was the right decision? We were relieved. And we were at Peace.

25 - BEAUTY-FULL

❖

Beauty, no matter where we live, work or go never ever leaves us. It is always there, even in the darkest places. All it needs to be released into our lives is for us to notice it, to lay our eyes or our thoughts on it. Then it grows. And then we notice more of it, and then a bit more and so on. And if we keep this up, several times a day for a few weeks, the beauty in our lives becomes the thing we see the most of. And, if we continue in this way and refuse to be thrown off course by other people or circumstances, before we know it our lives will be full of beauty. Beauty-*full*. And, this is all because we made the choice to notice it. To stop dwelling in the dull, the negative, the hard and the unfair, and to take a different path onwards and outwards, moving towards Peace.

Beauty is found in the oddest places and it's certainly not up to me to tell you where to look for it, but it's right there, at the end of your fingertips. In fact, have you looked at your fingertips lately? You see?

Aren't they unique?

Don't be afraid to start that small in your search for beauty. Your fingertips and hands are not insignificant; they are miraculous and they can help and heal. That is beauty. Now go, fill your boots with the stuff. It's everywhere.

26 - BREAKING THE CYCLE OF HURT

❖

I f you live any kind of life worthy of living, the chances are that you'll be hurt by a fellow human being, along the way. The hurt will invariably come out of left field and leave you feeling like you've been kicked in the face. It may also come from someone you trust and love deeply. It'll leave you in a state of shock, despair, sadness, and sorrow and, perhaps, even anger. Being hurt by another person is utterly, utterly wretched and there's very little you can do to be prepared for it when it happens, especially if you're unprepared in some way to deal with the feelings attached to it.

I am almost convinced that hurt has to happen to us all in some way, because the experience of it throws up so many different reactions in us that are all absolutely invaluable to pass on to others. I do, however, believe that we can control one aspect of the situation when this occurs – and that is how long it takes us to recover afterwards. I believe that our recovery time can shorten throughout our lifetimes, so that we can get to the point where we are hurt one moment and then in the next we have moved on and are back to joy. It takes practice to achieve this, and sometimes it takes more thought and effort than you would like, depending on how you were feeling prior to the betrayal. That said, it does become a muscle memory in your brain after a time. And, when used in conjunction with many of the other points in this book, it offers a life of great freedom.

Here are only three simple, but extremely powerful steps to freedom:

1. People may hurt you, but don't consciously seek to hurt them back.
2. Take nothing that anyone does personally.
3. Break the cycle *in an instant* by forgiving others.

I can hear you saying that it's unfortunate that there are steps in there such as take nothing 'personally' and practice forgiveness. And I understand, believe me, I do. I have been insulted with the best of them, but when you take nothing personally, you become impenetrable to hurt in a way that is vastly different from just putting up a front. Of course, you have to make the first move in all of this.

Which is also pretty shitty as you're the one who has been hurt for goodness' sake! Yes, I know, living a life of freedom takes a huge amount of effort on our part when we often really don't feel like it, but that's the deal. And the pay-off will blow your mind.

I can vividly recall the day the power of forgiveness blew my mind and set me free, thus breaking a cycle of hurt that was in my life. I was deeply entrenched in a legal battle that I didn't know how to handle. I had no idea what I was doing, what was going to happen and how the hell it would end up. I had just had a call from my lawyer who told me that there had been another 'swipe' taken by the opposite side and I had a choice to make. The choices you make in these sorts of situations are always the lesser of two evils (I've learned that much) and after making it and informing my lawyer, all I wanted to do was to hold my children, smell them because they smell of innocence, and never ever let them go. It just so happened that they were at the nursery that morning, but I knew I could start to get ready to go and get them by running a hot bath and warming up a bit as I was freezing cold.

The evening before I had finished reading *A Return to*

Love by Marianne Williamson. It's a book that advocates the practical application of love in every day life and reading it signalled change in my life for the better. As I read through the pages I could feel that she was explaining concepts that were important to me; I just got a feeling of freedom from reading what she had written, which I welcomed because I had felt trapped for so long. And so, that morning, after my bath, I found myself in the house alone, drying my leg off, and randomly saying out loud 'I love you and I hope you're OK' to the person who was orchestrating the action that was causing me pain. At that moment a huge weight was lifted from me. I know now that I had broken the cycle of hurt. Over the next few weeks and months, I worked on thoughts of forgiveness when this person came into my mind and sure enough with each consciously directed thought, the process got easier and easier, until today I am grateful for it.

Forgiving back then was (and still is) quite a process and I wasn't instantly living without fear, but I made the first step and the whole universe instantly conspired to make sure that it heard me and responded in kind.

Some moments stay with us: even all these years later, that simple act of drying my right leg is stamped indelibly in my brain. Why? Because that's when Peace came upon me.

27 - I WANT YOU TO KNOW SOMETHING

❖

You know what? *It. Is. Going. To. Be. Alright.* It's going to be better than alright. It's going to be wonderful. It's OK. It's *all* OK. Know what this chapter of your life *is* and what it is *not*. See the whole of it and not just the part that hurts. Acceptance of what is right now doesn't mean that it won't change. Everything changes because life is cyclical in all forms. We know that. We know that deeply. Let's make it convenient to remember it and not conveniently forget it and prolong the hurt.

It's already OK. It's already better. It's already wonderful. Make that your present moment right now and you'll immediately see the Peace in it.

28 - WHAT IS KINDNESS GOOD FOR?

❖

Kindness has made me feel like a doormat in the past. Really, what is the point in doing kind things and being a kind person if you're just going to be taken advantage of for trying? Well, I think it boils down to how we see Kindness as a quality in itself. If we are coming from the perspective that Kindness will make others like us more, or that it will help us to get what we want in some way then yes, it's wide open to be taken advantage of. But, if we're coming from the direction of Kindness as one of our greatest strengths, then we're opening the door for it take on a whole new meaning for us in ways we'd simply never imagined.

Once Kindness has morphed into strength within us, it then becomes Wisdom and *THAT* is where things get interesting. It's still possible to remember people's birthdays and help out with others' children, those acts of Kindness will never be wasted, but when we have a level of confidence in our ability to be kind then Wisdom flows through it. You've heard the saying 'you have to be cruel to be kind'. I *hate* that saying. I think it's trite and unfeeling. So instead I trust in the saying 'you have to be wise to be truly kind'. Wisdom within kindness helps us to make the really hard decisions in life. The ones that have some sort of consequence for others or for ourselves. The ones that possibly might be construed as less than helpful, but which we know are right and must be made. Wisdom helps us to see the long-term picture and not just focus on the short-term view. It delays gratification for the prize at the end of the journey. Parents need to be wise to be kind to their children. To see the long-term view in the midst of public tantrums and the mind-blowing sobbing that breaks your heart. But wisdom wins and the funny thing is that it won't necessarily be remembered as wisdom in you, but as kindness. Of course, you'll know that it's a magic mixture of both and that will bring you much Peace. It's certainly a road that has to be travelled. However rarely it's chosen by us.

29 - TO SETTLE OR TO SOAR?

❖

Robert and I went to see Ludovico Einaudi perform at Blenheim Palace, in Oxfordshire, on a warm and sunny June evening. Blenheim, if you've not been, is a magical place. Enormous, yet not too imposing; formal, but not stiff; and utterly beautiful from every vantage point. There was a rich calm in the air, which you could cut with a knife. It was like a mass meditation was taking place and everyone there was of the same mind, heart and soul (albeit, while enjoying glasses of iced cider and champagne on the grass in the setting English sun).

Einaudi, a 69-year-old Italian composer, took humbly to the stage and sat down at a Steinway piano. There were cameras on his hands as they touched the keys very gently and no matter how lightly he played, the sound resonated across the several thousand people gathered to hear him. He spoke very little, but one of the things he did say to the audience was that he loved us. To my left, I saw the moon in the sky above the entrance to the Palace; to my right, the sun was going down in a sea of red fire over the lakes. Swallows danced in the air above us, as Einaudi and his fellow musicians played with a passion that was translated to the audience as effortless.

That night the musicians soared. And we, as their audience, soared with them, such was their gift, and I felt overwhelming happiness as I witnessed it. While I was watching, I got caught up in thinking about life in general in a reflective and contemplative way. I realized that to soar in life, as those musicians clearly were doing, is actually far more Peace-full than to prevent ourselves from doing so. We think that there is great fear in stepping out of the box, but, in fact, when we've taken that step, our courage is rewarded and we are often filled with happiness. It's when we don't step forward, opting to settle instead, that the fear sets in. And there is no Peace in fear.

To settle or to soar? That is the question. I believe that for Peace to be in your life, you have to soar. Yes, it's true, you may find yourself higher than you've ever been before and that can be a little disconcerting, but the view will be spectacular.

30 - WHAT I SEE VERSUS WHAT YOU SEE

❖

I look at you and see you as the most valuable creature there ever was. You're a human being, you see, and all human beings are utterly precious in the most unfathomable ways. If I were Queen of the World, I would give you everything your heart ever wished for in the dead of night when you thought no one else was listening. I would ensure that your entire dreams came true immediately and that you never felt anything but Peace for the rest of your life. I would enjoy feeling free together with you because we would both know that we were free, free indeed. We would love everything and everyone unconditionally because it was the only thing we knew and we would be safe in that. There would be no fear in our loving.

If I were Queen of the World, I would be there on the front row to applaud your creativity. Or perhaps hear from you by email that you were going to receive the funding for your research. Maybe even that you were having a baby after two miscarriages or that you were leading a whole team of people into an unknown adventure.

I would see in you everything that you knew, felt and were certain you could be. I would see in you everything that you wanted to be or even just fancied trying for a bit.

So why do I have absolutely no trouble seeing all of these things for you? There's only one reason. I think you're worthy of them and you don't. Now you could argue with me that your history or previous circumstances don't allow you to feel very worthy right now. OK. Well, all those things I just mentioned will stay on hold until you do. Not to punish you even further, but just because there's no way in. It's not a question of creating perfection around us and in us so that we can then know Peace. It's a simple act of saying I am broken, I am in pain, I have been hurt and I am embarrassed. I am feeling shame. But I am still worthy. I may feel like half a human being right now, but I am *still* a human being and that is what makes me worthy. It is simple, almost too simple. But it is true. And it is powerful. When you recognize that, you will know Peace.

31 - SLEEP IN HEAVENLY PEACE

❖

This chapter is called 'Sleep in Heavenly Peace'. You'll probably recognize it as a line from a rather famous Christmas song and it happens to be the one that I sang to my children at bedtime when they were very small. It had a delicious calming effect on them, and me, and we all slept well. And the more I sang it to them, the more I thought about what sleeping in Heavenly Peace actually meant to me.

If there's one act of 'self care' that I'd wish we'd take more seriously it's that of sleeping well. I really don't think we understand just how fatigued we become when we experience a broken night's sleep for just a few days, let alone several weeks or even months on end. Insomnia can be brutal. I had it for a few months when I was a teenager and my form took waking up on the hour, every hour throughout the night. I realized then the importance of not just sleep, but good sleep. Deep sleep. Heavenly, Peace-full sleep.

We never stop. Our brains never really stop and our bodies certainly don't even when we are sleeping, so in order to stay in tip-top condition, we have to be able to rest well as often as we can. But how do we do that when our brains are constantly active? Well, the only answer I know of is to work on the process of stilling and quietening our thoughts in the lead-up to bedtime. This manifests itself in my life as no TV in the bedroom, no caffeine after a certain time in the day, no sugar after a certain time either, the most comfortable bed I can find, the softest linen and the right pillow for me. It also means that I try to create a sanctuary in my bedroom. I never write or blog from my bedroom. I have always done that from my desk (or the sofa when I was pregnant and couldn't fit behind my desk). I do check my email and social media from my bedroom, but it's never the last thing I do before turning out the light. That is reserved for reading. I read a great deal and have two or three books on the go at any one time. These books are invariably works of non-fiction so they tend to relax and inspire as opposed to excite and rev-up before bedtime. I also meditate, regularly. I began to meditate about three years ago and I could barely make it through 15 minutes of sitting still. Now I see that by sticking with the practice it has transformed my way of thinking and the way my brain works, too. It has also helped me to relax, not 'sweat the small stuff' and the upshot of this is that I sleep well. I sleep very well. I sleep in Heavenly Peace.

32 - CUT THE REFINED CRAP, GAIN THE CLARITY

❖

In March of 2015, I gave up eating sugar. I set myself a target of 60 days in which I would only get sugar from berries. Not from refined carbohydrates, refined or added sugars or any other fruit than the berries. The first few weeks were very strange as I realized the amount of preparation that I would need to do in order to complete the challenge. I found myself at a children's party at the start of the 60 days munching on a bag of rocket (arugula), as it was the only sugar-free food item I had to hand. Apart from the general sense of well-being, weight loss and glowing skin that I eventually gained from this experiment, I also got something else into the bargain that I hadn't counted on at all. I experienced the most extraordinary sense of clarity that I have ever had. Everything was clear to me. Meditation became easier, I was more productive and I was calmer. I started to understand myself a lot more. I forgave people for things that I'd harboured for years in the blink of an eye, never to look back. It was extraordinary.

This sense of clarity that I had gained was at once life changing and addictive. If a food group had been keeping this way of life from me, then I never wanted anything else to do with it. I saw the connection between my body and mind so very clearly – although I had previously known that they were inextricably linked, it was still startling. I never wanted the clarity to leave me, as when I was feeling clear, I was also at Peace.

I fell off the sugar wagon about three times during my 60 days and immediately got back on and forged ahead. And I have certainly introduced more fruit to my diet and had chocolate and other sugars since completing it. But you can never really go back to that way of eating, once you know what it's like on the other side. I didn't have to go on a fancy retreat miles from anywhere or have any sort of religious experience to gain the sort of clarity that I had always wanted to experience. By eliminating refined sugar from my diet, I eliminated something that I knew was very bad for me, had no nutritional value, was a substance that doctors had been discredited by the food industry giants for exposing and something that was in almost everything. It made me wonder how else my life and Peace had been disrupted by something I considered normal.

I'm choosier now, as I love what I saw on the other side of eating refined sugar. I found clarity. I saw Peace.

33 - YOUR DREAMS MAY CHANGE

❖

My husband and I have five-year old twins. My son dreams of being a train driver when he grows up and my daughter James Bond. Now just say that I tell them that those dreams they currently have for their future are set in stone. That they cannot change their dreams or hopes for the future. That my son, if he decides that he likes cars instead of trains, will not be able to make the switch, he has to stick with trains. What if I also tell my daughter that she will always be Bond (in itself no bad thing), but can never be 'M'? That even if she is dog-tired of rolling around on the tops of buildings with a gun strapped to her thigh, she will never be able to use her experience in the field to become the best 'M' there ever will be? Apart from Dame Judi Dench, of course! How does that sound to you? Does that seem right? Does that seem fair? Of course, if both my children will be happy being a train driver and Bond forever, then I will willingly share their happiness. But in reality, as people, as human beings, we evolve, grow and change our minds about things. What we want when we're five, in all likelihood, won't be what we want when we're 30. But we keep ourselves in self-created/self-sustained box-es, perhaps more than we actually realize.

We grow up with certain expectations of what we should be, do and say – often shaped by how our families, friends and peers perceive us. Sometimes, if we believe in these things, too, from an early age, we can find ourselves stuck in a box as we grow up, unable to move beyond a dream that no longer fits or suits us. Our dreams should always be allowed to move on, be allowed to grow, but they should also be allowed to die, if that's what's best for us – and when I say 'die', I mean that they should be allowed to leave us with much joy and absolutely zero regret, if they're not right for us any longer. We should never be at the mercy of our dreams failing to come true when they're no longer the best things for us. They may have been the best things for our parents, our teachers, our friends or our partners, but if they are not the best things for *us*, then we should be able to tell that to ourselves and have the cour-age to move on without fear of recrimination.

It may be that you have grown up with a dream that has grown organically with you – in which case that's great. Or it may be that you need to or want to make a startling change that will entail you totally throw those people around you who had no idea that you wanted to excel in that particular field. Whatever your dream is, decide to instil it with Peace and then make steps to follow it through, but do it in that order. It'll no doubt need you to be courageous, but with Peace at your side, you'll excel and that is what is needed to navigate through your life as your dreams change. It'll be glorious though. It always is when a person is living out his/her destiny. *Whatever* that may be.

34 - TAKE TIME OUT TO TRUST

❖

I f we've been around on this planet for any length of time and have had different sorts of experiences, then the chances are we've come across people who are not to be trusted. And our experiences with them can leave us very wary of trusting anybody else. So, who should you trust in this minefield of people who may have the potential to crap all over you? Well, if you have trouble sorting the wheat from the chaff, so to speak, when it comes to people, take a step back and decide to only trust one person for a while. Yourself. If you've had a bad experience with trust, you'll do well to take some time out of the trusting game for a few weeks or months and get your internal Sat Nav working again. This isn't about shutting down and blocking people from ever entering your heart or your life again, but more about recalibrating yourself after misjudging someone. And we all have done that. And we all need to take time out from time to time.

To put it simply, if you don't trust yourself to choose the right sort of people to be in your life, then you can end up choosing incorrectly and become surrounded by people who don't necessarily have your best interests at heart.

I've found that the times when I've trusted the wrong sorts of people are when I've been incredibly fearful of what the future holds. And, at those times, I was at my most vulnerable and lost. If I had only trusted myself enough, I would have known that spending precious, precious time just gathering both myself and my thoughts together would be invaluable and save a great deal of heartache later on down the line. So, don't berate yourself for making a seemingly bad choice. Just take a step back. Nurture your ability to trust yourself again. Get to know, really know, what you love and what you don't like that much. Nail down your thoughts and beliefs about the subjects that you are passionate about and have confidence in them. They are yours and they are valid. Knowing deep in your soul that you can trust yourself and your instincts about certain people in your life is an invaluable investment and one that brings immeasurable Peace. I promise it's true, as I, too, have made that investment in myself.

35 - LET IT BE

❖

Occasionally, when the veritable shit has hit the fan, we'll get a gut feeling that we need to let the situation be. Back away, take our hands off, pull back and withdraw. You get the picture. This can be one of the scariest things we ever choose to do – or not do. Personally, as someone who thinks she's pretty capable, NOT doing something, especially when a situation could clearly be made so much better by action, is extremely tough. More so, when the situation in question has people that I love and care for at the heart of it. But just because I *could* do something, it doesn't mean that I *should*.

Letting things 'be', instead of diving in and rescuing, enables others to grow and, especially in the case of children, it instils confidence. By throwing ourselves into the ring to help others, just because we can, we are effectively robbing them of that wonderful feeling we get when we know we've come through the other side of a horrid time. That means that they won't get to experience that visceral feeling of achievement. The one that gets us up out of bed the next day with the knowledge that we *can* do it. And, if they don't have that in their arsenal, how do they, in turn, pass it on? We won't be around forever. Knowing when to step in is, of course, a personal judgement call at all times, but I do believe it's possible to keep a watchful eye on proceedings without the other person ever knowing that we're doing so.

Courage is something that we all need to cultivate and unfortunately that only occurs in situations where courage is required. Letting it be doesn't mean we love less, but it does mean we love with a much broader outlook of what the human spirit is actually capable of (which is a tremendous amount and utterly miraculous if we did but know it). And sometimes we need to let things be, just so that others can gain or regain their Peace. Although this involves having to sit on our hands occasionally and bite our lips, I promise that it's worth it. Because the conversations that are then possible with the folk concerned, after the fact, will be extraordinary. And they may just lead to some new knowledge about ourselves, something that is priceless.

36 - VISION NEEDS A TRAVELLING PARTNER

❖

You've got vision. You're a person with a dream. The ambition you hold within you is a tremendous force, driving you forward. You want to make changes, not only in your life, but also in the lives of others. Things need to change and you're the person to do it. Your energy is unstoppable and you never tire. You can see your vision so very clearly as it plays out in your imagination and there's nothing in you that doubts that any part of it won't happen. You've got the funding, the team, the materials, the website, the permission and the go-ahead. You got the job, the promotion, the contract or the role. Everything is there waiting for you to move. But you are frozen to the spot! Paralyzed with fear to the extent that you can't make head or tail of anything that is being said to you. Your energy is leaking out of you like a tap turned on full and what you'd really like to do is sleep. The doubts creep in. Where's your creative streak disappeared to? What's happened to your edge? They thought you were the 'one' (whatever that means).

Let me make it clear that I believe vision in people should be encouraged. We get so enthused by those people with vision that we invariably follow them, We are inspired by them and often want to be just like them. People with vision are intoxicating, exciting and make us feel like anything is possible.

The reality is anything *is* possible. We've seen that time and time again throughout history with the good, the bad and the truly heinous.

But know this (and this is the point of this chapter and the bit that is not taught often enough): vision requires an equal partner and that partner is courage. When you have vision, but lack courage, you'll last a very short amount of time when it comes to following through. It's just not enough to believe in what you're doing. Belief alone will not get you through those times when you actually have to be really, really courageous. But how does this need for courage manifest itself in us? Here are just a few examples:

- You may need to be vulnerable.
- You may need to show a part of yourself you've kept previously hidden.

- You may need to disagree with the majority, some-one you respect or dislike.
- You may need to speak up.
- You may need to defend others.
- You may need to defend yourself.
- You may be the only one left standing.
- You may have to wait a long time for your opportu-nity to arise.
- You may face abuse, lies and smears.
- You may have to keep going and going and going and going.

Whatever your vision, decide right now to make it an equal partner with courage because the two go hand in hand. They are best friends, soulmates, the ying to the other's yang. Then, when the path to seeing your vision come alive is rocky, you'll at least have Peace. During those times of uncertainty, Peace will be your very best travel-ling partner and will ensure that you never turn back, but keep right on going.

37 – PERFECTION, THE GREAT EXCUSE

❖

When I hear a person say that they're waiting until everything is 'perfect' before they make a start, launch a product, change career, have a baby, write a book, and so on, then I know that it will never get done. Waiting for things to be 'perfect' is a great excuse for not getting the thing done at all, because whether you know it, consciously or unconsciously, that time will *never* come. Waiting for perfection is simply waiting for fear to pass and if you wait for that to go, fear will stay around with a tenacity that will shock you. If all your bases have been covered, all your preparations made and if there is nothing more that you can do, then you absolutely have to throw your hat into the ring immediately. Do you risk failure? Yep, and that's fear speaking through you again. Shut it up and walk away. Infuriate it by casting it aside.

Decide instead to walk in love, which, in turn, becomes courage, which then leads to boldness, which reveals itself as dreams coming true and miracles you'd only ever dreamed of.

Will it be perfect? Yes. It will. Perfect because it can only have come from you and you are perfection. Flaws and all.

38 - YOUR DREAMS SHOULD MAKE YOU HAPPY

❖

You have a dream for your life. How does it feel? Does it make you stressed or anxious? Does it make you feel nervous in an unconfident way? Do you feel lost within it and unable to see what steps should be taken next? If this is the case and this sort of situation has been going on for any length of time then I would hazard a very good guess that due to the lack of Peace you are feeling about this, you should seriously think about pursuing another path.

Your dreams are not here, and have never been here, to taunt you with their seeming lack of ability to come true. A dream is not by definition a *true* dream unless it comes to pass. And I'm not talking about the dreams we have at night times, but those dreams and pictures you have in your mind when you're on the Tube going in to work or at your desk sorting through emails from the weekend but your mind isn't really on the job. Those sorts of dreams are the ones I'm talking about and their entire modus operandi is to come true. And, along the way, you can tell if you're on the right track with them because two things will happen in sequence – you'll feel at Peace throughout the journey of seeing this dream being realized, no matter how 'hard' it gets. 'Hard' being a relative term, as if you love something then hard isn't really hard at all. And then you'll find that those dreams will propel you forward along the way. You won't be in the dark about what steps to take next for very long at all. The path will become clear to you through inspiration of some sort or an idea striking you at the most surprising of moments. You'll get excited about this next step and things will fall into place in a way that makes you feel like you knew this route all along.

Your dreams and ambitions are absolutely there to make you happy. And through that happiness comes Peace and also the realization that miracles happen every single day. In fact, you'll get so used to them you'll almost be able to tell when they are about to happen. This is being in alignment. This is where we are all meant to be every second of the day. This is where we need to get back to. And this is where Peace is.

39 - WE BECOME WHAT WE THINK ABOUT

❖

Our thoughts are important. Our thoughts can actualize into actions. Our thoughts can have consequences – negative or positive. And we don't get to send mixed messages out there and live a life of Peace. The thoughts we put out there, positive or negative, may not always come back to us like for like, but come back to us they will. And they'll come back to us in the *spirit and intention* in which they were sent out. If you don't know this, then it can be almost impossible to recognize what is going on in our lives and the part that *we* have played in it. Especially if there is a delay in the time between you sending something out there with your thoughts, words or actions and how your life unfolds afterwards and over time. This is not a punishment as such, but it is a law and it's there so that there are checks and balances in place and so that we can live in Peace. Otherwise we'd descend into even more chaos than there is right now.

It starts with the thought. The thought becomes a feeling, sometimes instantaneously. The feeling then becomes an action. And based upon what action we take that becomes the life we experience. This means that at our disposal is a very large way of controlling how we experience life. If only we took seriously the chain of events that begins with the thought. Because the thought is the thing: it's the thing that stands between Peace and us.

40 - FEAR VERSUS COURAGE

❖

'Dare to Dream?' Why are we told that? 'Dare' – Why use that particular word? If it weren't used, everything would be a whole lot easier, wouldn't it? But it's there for a reason. It's there because the sages knew very early on that one of the things we're most frightened of is failure. So life 'dares' us to dream. It doesn't taunt us or tease us, but it asks something of us; it asks us to stare our current situation in the face and tell it that, because of our courage, it shall change. And stepping into courage first – being the one who chooses to make a move happen – sets the wheels of Peace in motion.

Fear is a bully and a thief. Whole lives can be, and indeed are, thwarted by fearing what may or may not happen in the future. Fear tells you that you are ridiculous to think that the ambitions you have for your life stand any chance of happening and by doing so it adds a lovely dollop of shame to the mix that it's already piled on your head. Fear exists to squash any kind of desire in you for anything different – whether that be a set of beliefs or a standard of living, or anything else in-between. Fear is there to make you feel falsely safe within it by slowly eating away at every part of you that contains life. It does it so well that you'd hardly notice it. Except, that is, when you've seen the opposite of fear – love – at work you won't ever be able to go back to the prison you were once in. When that happens, put simply as you've seen the light (love), the thought of going back into darkness is too much to bear. You simply won't do it; you will not go there again. You'll muster all the courage you have to stay in the light, to keep on living from a loving intention, instead of one driven by fear, anxiety, anger and eventual apathy for life itself.

I believe in you, no matter where you are. And I believe that you'll dare to dream because the alternative doesn't bear thinking about. You'd rather *'fail'* every day of your life than have to face the fact that you just didn't 'give it a go' because you felt you couldn't. There is no longer any room for 'just didn't' in your vocabulary, life or heart. And a life half lived is not on your radar. You are now a 'just did it' person, who will then become a 'just changed it' person. People who change things, change lives and they usually start with their own. How do they do this? – by daring to dream and landing fear a right hook square between the eyes in the process. And boy does that feel good!

41 - DON'T FIGHT IT, JUST ALLOW IT

❖

Allowing tough times to play out is one of the best ways to find Peace. By this, I mean that when something significant happens, before your sense of shock, calm or rationale kicks in, and before you start trying to think 'straight', just allow your immediate response – your gut reaction or thoughts – to wash right over you. Don't fight them and don't question them. Don't change them and don't judge them. Just let them be. Don't engage with them. Take a breath and step back. This will, without doubt, be one of the hardest roads to Peace that I personally feel you will take, but by allowing those feelings, which, most of the time, scare the living crap out of you to ebb and flow, you will let them run their natural course and, in turn, shorten the time that they are with you. You will then be able to 'let go' more successfully because you haven't done what we all do naturally, and that is grab onto the emotion. The moment we do that – because we see safety in it, secretly enjoy a sense of drama or just can't help but feel a victim, for example – we give those emotions credence for as long as we keep our attention on them. This allows fear to begin working in our lives. And it will grow like germs in a Petri dish until we consciously step in to quash it.

So how do we take that moment or that breath that enables us to step back and allow our gut reaction and thoughts to just be?

- Don't do a thing: not even think.
- Allow any feelings or thoughts that do come to roll in without a struggle.
- And then take a very deep breath.

Breath is life, as we have discussed before in Chapter 1 'Every breath you take'. And, within the breath that you take in that moment, you're making a conscious decision to step away from taking your place on the terrible roller-coaster that fear would have you sit on for all eternity, if it could. Put simply, you do not have to live in fear; you can choose to live in love. Love won't give fear any more acknowledgement than it needs to serve love's own purpose. And in doing that, in that instant, you will know Peace. It will take some practice to keep Peace from being whipped away by fear, but you will know it. And once you know it, you'll actively seek Peace out and, you will find it.

42 - YOUR FUTURE IS NOW

❖

Do you want to know what your future will look like? I thought you might. We have all, at some time or another, wanted to see what our future holds in store for us. And, like most things, I've realized, the simplest way to find out is to look right beneath our noses. If you want to see your future, then look at your today. What are you saying right now? What are you thinking right now? What are you feeling right now? What situation are you 'seeing' right now? There are several ways to see situation after all. If you take a look, and you don't like what you see, then change it to something you do like. Because quite simply, if you change your today, you'll change your tomorrow. Life is more simple than we think. And, there are only two factors worth giving our attention to, in my opinion: love or fear.

Once we take the route governed by love, we'll see Peace, as well as the brightest future imaginable. Created by us, for us, out of pure love.

43 - YOU NEVER, EVER, EVER HAVE TO CONVINCE ANYONE OF ANYTHING

❖

You never, ever, ever have to convince anyone of anything. Ever. I'm telling you this. It's true. That's a relief, isn't it? To know that you don't have to persuade any other person on this planet to like the things you like. Or to love the people you love. To try and persuade them to believe in the dreams you believe in or see the things you see in your mind's eye. I would take this one step further and suggest that you guard your goals, visions and loves with all of your might, while you yourself get to know them. What I mean by this is that your wishes and thoughts make you absolutely unique and beautiful. They change you and have the power to change others, so guard them with your life. Don't seek approval; you may rarely get it in the form that you seek. But set your own personal standards by which to live your life. It's much more satisfying.

Imagine what the world would be like if we all were so secure in our dreams and ambitions that we never felt the need to seek approval from anyone else. We just simply went about our lives fulfilling them.

It would be at Peace that is what it would be like.

44 - THE PEOPLE PRISON

❖

What will they say? What will they think? What will they tell others?

The reality is that we don't speak, act, work, create, eat or live the way we could or should, because we're being held in a prison, the People Prison. Let me tell you something. It's possible, not probable (I'm the eternal optimist), but *possible* that people will talk about you behind your back, at some point in your life. And the things they say won't be exactly what you'd ideally want them to be saying. It's also possible that, from time to time, others will have thoughts and opinions about you that are very far removed from who you know you actually are. You may never know that they have these thoughts and opinions, but, without a doubt, they will absolutely inform how you interact with each other because we're all connected. But will the fact that other people are making the business of your business their business, stop you from being all that you can be? Will you be left to rot in the prison made by other people? Where other people get to decide which keys they hold to your life? It's your choice.

A strange thing happens when you begin to live your truth (public opinion be damned), you start to attract exactly the right sort of people for you to you. People are all attracted to each other by the signals we send out to each other (the connection thing again), so by sending out the ones that bear most resemblance to who and what you are, you'll find yourself surrounded by the best people for you and your life. The 'Toxics', as I call them, may hang around for a wee bit after you've made your conscious attraction decision, but you'll be so happy and joy-full that you'll barely notice them. You'll be free. Free from the People Prison and free to soar. And, that is what our dearest friends allow us to do. They allow and want us to soar. They want us up there riding on the thermals and living our big lives. Not stuck down here, at the mercy of thoughts, comments, judgements and gossip. It can be tough to believe that all we have to do is shake off the shackles and break free of the People Prison to go in search of pastures new and that actually we can do that in an instant with just a change in the direction of our thoughts. But we can. And there is great Peace to be found outside of that prison made by people. Break free of the People Prison and you'll embrace Peace.

45 - DEEP & TRUE CONFIDENCE

❖

There's something magic about people who have deep and true confidence. It's such a relief to see them in action. Through being confident, they seem to release the rest of us to be more ourselves. They don't wrestle for airtime or attention and have no sense of having to rush things. They just are. In the most delicious and comforting way. They have such a secure sense of self that in among a sea of brashness they are the ones we notice. They are the ones who have the ability to alter the atmosphere in a room.

So in a world in which personal worth is often measured by 'likes', 'followers', 'hits', 'views' and regulated by 'trolls', what is confidence? Because when worth is measured in such an extreme way, as it so often is these days, how can we tell when true confidence has developed within us?

Most of us acknowledge that confidence isn't the same as arrogance. It isn't having the loudest voice or being the most controversial or adversarial speaker. It's not the person who has done the most, but rather the person who *is* the most. Not the cleverest person, but the one who recognizes that s/he will never stop learning and is not just OK with that but excited by it.

What is confidence? Confidence is humble. It's funny. It's gentle. It's kind. It's inventive. It's energetic. It deeply understands. It's non-judgemental. It's very passionate. It's focused. It's inspiringly ambitious. It trusts the process of living in love rather than fear.

Grow and nurture your confidence because when you truly have it, it's an invaluable gift and not one that should be given up without a fight. You see, they'll come for it, those Toxics, the people who want to knock you down, believe me they will. But don't let them. With confidence comes the Peace that will see you through. So, don't give it up. It's invaluable.

46 -THERE IS FREEDOM IN FORGIVENESS

❖

Forgiveness.

One of the most misunderstood concepts, philosophies and actions around. To forgive someone, when s/he has done something to you that has hurt you is, even today, with all the knowledge we have at our disposal, often viewed as a sign of weakness. But the longer we prolong the myth that 'getting mad' and 'getting even' is the best way forward, the longer we keep the miraculous life-, body- and mind-changing power of forgiveness out in the cold. Forgiveness is an incredibly powerful path to Peace. When you forgive someone, you're not letting that person off the hook, I promise you. What you're doing, instead, is freeing yourself. The other person will still have to deal with what s/he has done and life has an extraordinary way of coming back to bite you. By forgiving, you are choosing to free *YOURSELF* from a toxicity made up of hate, anger, disquiet, bitterness, anxiety, fear and other negative emotions, the very signs of non-forgiveness in people. It may seem a shitty deal for you to be the one who has to forgive THEM, the perpetrators of the actions that have hurt or damaged you in some way, but the alternative is really not worth thinking about for any serious length of time as it will only rebound on you.

People age physically when they are unable to forgive; they curl inwards on themselves due to past and unresolved hurts. But you'll be able to recognize people who hold no anger towards other people by their openness, their carefree and confident way of being with you. They are not afraid of getting hurt again because they know that if that happens, they can forgive and get back on track.

Imagine the cleanest, bluest ocean in a heavenly place on earth. The water is full of sea life, plants and coral. You can see your feet when you walk in the water, like you are staring through glass. The sea is as warm as a bath with the most perfect of breezes caressing your skin. Would you ever consciously empty a tanker of crude oil into that water? Knowing you would have to watch it as it slowly but very, very surely seeped into the water and coloured everything in its path with its thick, toxic darkness? Changing it beyond all recognition from something so life giving to something in which everything would have to struggle to survive? Would you do that? Non-forgiveness is the same as that oil. It damages an otherwise beautiful life from the inside out.

Don't ever mistake the act of forgiveness as weakness on your part. It's not about absolving people of their guilt or about setting them free from owning up to their actions. It's about setting yourself free. You have your own life to create and live and the beauty of that ocean is yours to swim in if you keep it from being infected.

In choosing forgiveness, you are setting up boundaries for living your life that won't be crossed again and that is exactly how we avoid the same things happening over and over. Forgiveness also allows you to live a life that will be magnificent as it is not contaminated by negativity. And each time you forgive someone (and yourself, don't forget yourself), the healing water of that warm turquoise blue ocean will wash over you once more and will remind you, in the most loving and luxurious way, of the life you that are truly meant to be living. Joy-full, beauty-full, abundant, fun. Not stuck, angry, lacking and unhappy.

Have courage in this. It does work. Forgiveness will bring you Peace and it will also empower you. Quite a life-changing combination and one that is not just beautiful to experience, but also one that's beautiful to behold.

47 - THE BROKEN PEOPLE

❖

One thing that will remain true, until the end of our time on earth, is that each and every person we stumble across, ourselves included, will have been broken in some way or another at some time or other. We may have been dropped (metaphorically) from a great height through neglect, abuse, and lack of interest or bullying when we were young. We may have been tiny victims of circumstances that ate away at the souls we arrived here with to be replaced by ones that fitted the world around us a little better. Our breakages may have happened later on in life as we hit our teens or young adulthood. Maybe our childhood dreams all worked out for us and it was in our twenties or thirties that everything fell apart and we ripped a bit at the seams

I believe that pain is relative and I also believe that perspective is needed when we are in pain and that some situations are undoubtedly more serious and life altering than others. But the fact remains that most of us are broken in some way. Being broken doesn't mean that we can't be fixed. In fact, the rebuilding of ourselves, if done correctly, can and will make us titans of love, compassion and an abundant life. But it does mean that when we meet someone, we might do well to remember, just for a split second, that they also will have been broken at some point, or may even be breaking right at that moment.

By remembering this during our daily dealings with people, we are not excusing their bad behaviour or meanness but just rising above it and living on another level, a level in which wisdom presides and a distinct lack of ego is the norm. Peace is in abundance there, of course, and that allows us to spread it liberally around to each and every person who crosses our paths. In doing this we are changing the world for the better – and what higher calling is there, really? If we lead our lives in Peace, wisdom and love, people will be drawn to us like moths to flames. We're all broken; therefore we're all the same. We all need love, so never be afraid to give it liberally.

THAT is Peace on earth at work.

48 - WARRIOR VERSUS WORRIER

❖

It's really interesting to me that in the English language, two words so diametrically opposed to each other in meaning, look, sound and are spelled in almost exactly the same ways. When I hear people say, 'Oh, I'm such a worrier' – and it happens a lot – each and every time, a shiver runs down my spine. This isn't me being dramatic. I'm being absolutely serious. Shall I tell you why? Because these self-professed worriers are wasting their lives, yes their *lives*, on a practice that is based in futility. And, therefore, is a complete waste of time. In all probability, the things they are worrying about, most probably, haven't happened. They don't exist yet. So there is NOTHING to worry about. Literally, nothing there.

Worry can come at you from a situation that you may be finding hard to bear – for example, you or someone close to you may be ill, you may be going through a break up or in fear of losing your job. But worrying about such things is the least effective way of dealing with these kinds of debilitating circumstances. Worry destroys us and is ineffectual. Making us useless at the very time we need to be at our most clear, loving, strong and positive.

So choose now to create a new outcome by a change of thinking, Instead of being a self-professed Worrier, become a 'Warrior'. Picture a new ending that is free from anxiety. Dare to dream of a different answer or outcome. You may get it, you may not, or you may get something better, but at least you're trying and you'll have had a much greater and probably lighter journey, if you're not burdened by worry.

Worry can and does make you physically sick. Worry can be your identity and some people feel safe in worry. But they're being short changed. Short changed on their entire lives. Worry makes your head hurt and your bones weary and is, in all probability, based in something that most probably doesn't even exist yet. When put that way, it seems like the oddest way to spend time, but we do. We all do it, all of the time. And worry is based in fear when love isn't.

So I say, choose love. Every. Single. Time. And drop me an email to <u>cherry@cherrymenlove.com</u> with the tales of the miracles that will follow the best choice you could make for your life.

49 - YOU, THE CURATOR

❖

When we think of a 'curator', art galleries or museums immediately spring to mind. But did you know that you could – and should – curate your own life in much the same way? You see you have a choice, a great deal of the time, as to what you bring into your life.

If we're using the gallery analogy, when you visit you are usually seeing the work of a curator, who will usually have a great deal of academic achievements under his/her belt and will do a tremendous amount of research into the works that he or she is selecting. And that word *'selecting'* is absolutely vital for us to grasp hold of when we are talking about what we allow to hang on the walls of our own lives.

The great majority of us do have choices. We get to decide whom we allow into our lives on an emotional and physical level. We are able to decide, over time, where we live. And, a great many of us have a choice as to where we work. The great majority of us can also choose whom to marry or whether or not to have children. We get to pick restaurants, friends, holidays, hobbies and a vast number of things that go into making up our entire lives. They are our choices. It's when we stop remembering that so much of our lives are ours to curate that we let go of what's crucial. Then, our lives become an amalgamation of everyone else's and that's what we end up living. This is what breeds in us a sense of enormous dissatisfaction over time. We look at our lives and think 'this isn't where I'm meant to be', 'how did I get to this point?' When were we told to let go of the responsibility of curating our own lives?

Our lives, although they appear to go by in the blink of an eye, are lasting longer and longer, the healthier we get. We now have many years to create something that we love and we should, from the earliest opportunity, begin to create and curate something we can enjoy and love, no matter how far that journey may take us. It is a tremendously empowered way to live our lives and it's astounding how few of us truly know that we have a choice as to who we invite in, what we have and where we place things in the gallery that is actually our precious, precious time here on earth.

Being the true curator of your own life brings much Peace with it. You know that what you see only you are responsible for putting there. And when you know this, you also know that you are 'capable' of changing anything that you're not happy or comfortable with. 'Capable' is a word that I love. When you know you're capable you have Peace. And when you have Peace, you'll create the most terrific life/gallery/collection that you could ever have wished for.

50 - WHY DO WE HAVE TO CHOOSE?

❖

For the longest time I struggled to incorporate my love of the lifestyle genre, which I had blogged and been published in, with the deep passion for the more spiritual side of my life. I've been told many, many times by people in the media that I have to be specific with what I do. I have to be a certain type of person or my audience won't *get it*. Get what? There's nothing to get. I love it all. I love growing roses, cooking supper and reading books by Deepak Chopra AND Tim Ferris. I love finding a new fabric softener, a gorgeous silk scarf to tie around my head AND meditation. I love the caftan I bought for our family holiday and I love the Peace and tranquillity of Classic FM late at night. I love packing orders for my shop and curating new collections alongside writing blog posts. I write, I photograph, I style, I connect with others, I forge relationships, I source opportunities, I update my own website, I build my own web shop. The list goes on. Nothing is mutually exclusive when I love it. It's all just so interesting to me that I want to tell people, but most of all I want to do these things, experience them for myself.

I am all of these facets and all of these loves. Some are more important to me than others but no one is asking me to choose between one or the other any more. And no one is asking you to choose. Do it all if you want to or just do one thing. Be at Peace with being prolific. I am free and you are free to be all and everything that you can dream of being. And it's delicious.

You and I are free to soar and not to settle. We are free to be one version of ourselves one year and another the next. Our lives are moveable feasts because we are human and I am finally very comfortable with that, indeed. It is so exciting, the whole world and everything in it has opened up to me. Dare to find the place where you would be most free. Dare to move towards that space. Dare to think about soaring and not settling even if that kind of thinking takes you completely out of your comfort zone. Sometimes stepping out of our comfort zone immediately brings us in to total alignment with life. And we know that with alignment comes great Peace. And it's not as scary as you think above the trees and out of that metaphorical Forest of Fear. In fact it's lighter and closer to the sun. It's closer to love, full of deep Peace and there's room for everyone.

51 - ALIGNMENT BREEDS EXCELLENCE

❖

The older I get, and the longer I'm here, the more I believe in the power of alignment. Being in alignment to me means that my intentions, my thoughts, my heart and, therefore, my actions are all in the right place. I'm not making choices based on the needs of my ego: instead, my intention in doing the things I want to do is to add to my life and the lives of others, rather than taking away from either them or me. To add positive value, to make a good difference, to teach, to inspire, to love, to have fun – those elements are my focus when I am in alignment. I know the moment I go out of alignment as everything is suddenly a chore.

Being in alignment is not a chore and it takes very little effort from us to acquire exactly what we want and are focusing on. We are 'in the zone', 'going with the flow' or just simply having the time of our lives. You also trust time a lot more when you're in alignment. And, by that I mean that when we are using force to get things done, we often feel that time is not on our side. We feel rushed, confused, in a panic and totally unconfident about what we're doing. And this sense of what is essentially fear within our lives can lead us to make some devastating choices.

I remember working myself into the ground at one point in my life because I believed that only I could hold things together. I had a husband recovering from cancer, a pair of much-loved but demanding one-year-old twins to take care of, staff to pay, a book to write and a devastating situation with someone I had worked with and cared a great deal for. And all of these people from different parts of my life were vying for my attention and also relying on me to make sure everything would be OK. What I should have done was stop when it got too much, taken a moment and sat down to clearly prioritize what was most essential and important for me to take care of. What I should have done was spoken to more people and asked for help. What I should *not* have done was think that it was at all possible for me to be in perfect alignment when I was feeling quite so stretched.

Alignment doesn't stretch you until you don't know if you're coming or going. Alignment doesn't allow you to do lots of different things poorly instead of a few things excellently. Alignment breeds excellence. But we have to lose the fear of loss and step into it. If I could have that time of my life over again, I would take so many more people up on their offers of help and time. I would let go of my own expectations of myself as a Super Human – my ego – and admit that I just wanted to be with my husband and children until we were all stronger. I wouldn't have taken on a battle waged by someone desperate for my attention; instead I would have chosen to be in alignment with the situation, rather than caught up in its rapids. I would have trusted that my destiny would still have been fulfilled without the use of so much forceful effort. There is absolutely no Peace in forceful effort. None at all. Ever.

We may think we're being pro-active and industrious when we use so much effort, but are we mistaking what are Type A personality traits with the fact that we just can't find the courage to let go and trust the power of alignment? Perhaps. What I can tell you is that a beautiful journey down a softly winding river in a comfortable boat on a delicious summer's day is much more preferable than a stomach-churning race down the rapids in a punctured rubber ring. You get to see the scenery for a start. And I've made a promise never to miss the scenery again. It's just too beautiful.

What about you? Are you stretched out of alignment right now? If you are I beg you to stop just for a short time today. Get yourself alone somewhere and do what I wished I had done. Breathe, make a list of those priorities that are closest to your heart and ask for help. It won't make everything perfect immediately but it's a start. A start on the road back towards Peace.

52 - KEEP CALM AND SEE PEACE

❖

In the past, when people used to extol the virtues of being calm in most situations, I often wondered if that wasn't a rather boring way to live. But, over time, I have found that calmness and having a calming influence brings you heaven on earth. It works when I am calm with my children; it works when I create a sense of calm in my home; and it works in moments of extreme stress for me personally to create a sense of calmness. It is almost like a magical spell from the writing of C.S. Lewis or J.K. Rowling: it's that powerful and that quick to take effect.

I used to believe that those people who were always calm either had no passion in them or were just dead inside. And it's true, there are people who are like that. Yet, what I have come to realize is that having a sense of calm in no way denotes a lack of life. In fact, I believe that it means you see life very clearly indeed. Practising the art of being calm while remaining compassionate, passionate and empathetic gives you a certain confidence that isn't thrown off course at a moment's notice, plunging you into chaotic emotions or allowing you to be blindsided by an event that you hadn't planned for.

I recognized the Peace within the power of calm very recently. I received an email, via a friend, from a person who is just absolutely toxic to me in all of their actions. I feel no malice towards them whatsoever, but it is quite disturbing the lengths to which that person to will go to disrupt my Peace. And I think we do have to accept that there are those types of people out there, although they are most certainly not in the majority. Anyway, I thought the timing of this email was absolute perfection, as here I am writing a book about the power of having Peace in your life and yet enter stage right someone from my past, who once undermined my Peace, still hell-bent on destroying it through the same threats and untruths. This time, however, I noticed that instead of freaking out, I was able to draw on the truth, as I know it. That being, my Peace is a ship that cannot be rocked and certainly not sunk. That no matter what happens beneath the water, I sail on calm, clear and utterly beautiful seas. And that I have a choice to sail towards a storm – but, if I do that, then I mustn't complain if I hit the rocks. I just need to steer my course, to keep the metaphorically delicious view I have of the land in my sight and enjoy the journey with a glass of fizz and my supper.

That is what keeping a sense of calm is all about to me, in a life that is full of passion and dreams and loves. But achieving and maintaining that calm, isn't about entertaining the drama of another who is on a different journey. Because that way is not helpful and that way is not the path to Peace.

53 - IT STARTS WITH YOU

S ome people feel that the world owes them a great deal more than they are currently receiving, and some believe that they don't wield that much power over their own lives. And possibly far too many people believe that to spend so much time focusing on themselves and their own well-being is exceedingly selfish – when it's not, it's actually exceedingly *vital*.

It's very difficult to accept, when we are feeling utterly devastated by life, that the process of rebuilding has to begin within ourselves, that it is pretty much solely down to us to make that decision to move forward, no matter how weak we may feel. To take our own futures by the hand and gently pull them back on to their feet can take an extraordinary amount of effort and mental time. But it absolutely has to be done if we're to stand a chance of being truly healed of the devastation that can occur during our lives. It has to be our choice in the end to do this. We will undoubtedly need the support of others, but they cannot make this choice for us.

This issue was something that I personally grappled with for a long time. I desperately wanted rescuing; I didn't believe that all I needed, I already had. And yet, it was there all along, just very well hidden. The longer I looked for the metaphorical knight in shining armour, the longer I kept true strength and Peace at bay. The truth is until it was *my* decision to make a different choice with my life, my Peace and my strength were borrowed from others and no one can do that forever. That situation is simply not sustainable. It's scary stepping out on our own, especially when we've got a series of *perceived* failures (adventures) racked up against our names. But when we can transform a vision of failure into a vision of a past adventure, that's when we can move forward. It's baby steps at first, but I promise you that you'll know deep in your soul that it's YOU that is moving forward bravely. You in all your broken, weak and tiny glory perhaps, but at least it's you and not someone else doing it for you. And that knowledge brings so much Peace.

54 - PEACE IN THE IMPOSSIBLE

❖

Everything that you see around you in existence today started life as a thought. And a great many of those thoughts, when they were spoken out loud to other people, were labelled as impossible. Erase the word 'impossible' from your memory and from your vocabulary. Never allow yourself to be told that something is impossible, when you can see it clearly in your mind's eye. Because by virtue of the fact that you can see it, you can bring it to pass. But don't dwell on or, God forbid, worry about the method in which it will come to pass. Not knowing how something will happen has a tendency to bug the life out of some people and they get so hung up on the how, that their focus leaves them and they forever remain in the waiting room of that event. It doesn't happen.

Instead, allow yourself to get caught up in the feeling of sheer beauty that will be yours when you do finally see this 'impossibility' take shape before your eyes. Revel in the excitement of not knowing how it will occur. Allow the feeling of Peace to replace the feeling of impossible in your life. All you have to do is see it, believe it and receive it. The route it takes is not up to you and not your concern. You see? The world is perfect. While you have seen, believed and are simply waiting to receive, you can then get on with another project to save you from waiting around. The world works perfectly and in divine order if we'd only allow it to. And when we do allow it to we find great Peace.

55 - VERBAL ANNIHILATION

❖

Think about this for a moment: if you were to verbalize and speak aloud to another person the extreme/negative thoughts that run through your head about *yourself*, you'd most probably be accused of verbal assault. So why are we so accepting of speaking to ourselves in this way? Why do we verbally annihilate ourselves?

The stream of consciousness that runs through our minds and makes reference to ourselves is extraordinary in its negativity. Even if the thoughts are fleeting, the compounding nature of them eventually means that those thoughts shape and become who we are. They become what we present to the world around us. They become what we achieve with our life and our dreams. And by verbally annihilating ourselves for the greater part of the day through our thoughts, Peace is one of the last things we'll achieve. And yet for our well-being a sense of Peace is absolutely vital. How do we achieve this? Well, I'll be honest – it can be tricky to start with. But if you take notice of what your thoughts are about yourself in just one day, many will probably not be the sort of thing that you would say to a stranger, let alone a friend. So, ask yourselves then, why on earth are you saying them to yourself? Write down the thoughts you have about yourself and read them at the end of the day. I have a feeling you'll be absolutely shocked; not only by their sheer brutality, but also by the vast range of topics that they cover. Intellect, body shape, looks, hair, skin, job, position in job, upbringing, education, car, clothes, salary, fear, your dreams, your desires. You get the picture.

When thoughts go through our minds, if we are the only ones to hear them, they can be held captive there. There's no filter and, quite frankly, we're not always the best judges of what we should believe about ourselves. Those thoughts are often pernicious and do an incredible amount of damage when left unchecked over time. Ugh, if only there was a mechanism in our brains that would immediately switch these thoughts into positive thoughts the moment they got going. But, as we don't have that, it's up to us to do it ourselves. So rather than, 'I'm not smart enough for this', try 'right, this may be hard for me at first, but I'm giving it a go and I'll do my best'.

And instead of, 'Why have I let my body get so out of shape. It disgusts me', try 'OK, I've had children and they are healthy, so my body has done something pretty wonderful. I'll take a look at what I'm eating and if I'm moving enough this evening. But right now I'm late for work and I need my body to be on my side right now. Thank you body for standing strong with me. We can do this. I love you' This will feel slightly ridiculous and contrived at first. But it's something that is immensely powerful. Try it for a month. It'll be strange, I promise you, but then – be prepared for everything to change for the better. It will, I promise you.

56 - HEADING DOWN THE DRAIN

❖

Have you ever left the company of a person feeling absolutely drained? Devoid of all life like your actual blood has been sucked by their awfully negative attitude? Gracious, I have!! It can be pretty hard to spot these folk at first, as they're certainly not offensive; they're just draining, but that in itself is a problem. Some people get a strange kick out of immediately diffusing any enthusiasm in a room once it starts to raise its head. This is fear incarnate on their part and thoroughly controlling too. It may not be done consciously and, therefore, there's nobody to blame. All I can say is if it's someone you care about or someone you have no choice other than to have in your life, then stay your course.

Trust in enthusiasm because I can tell you that very little gets done without it. Trust in passion because it gives life its colour and a lot of draining people can prefer to live in a world of grey. Trust in spontaneity because when your gut tells you to do something, it's not often wrong. Don't fear people who drain you or you'll end up responding to them entirely inappropriately and that's not helpful to anyone. Just don't fear yourself. Trust yourself instead. Be at Peace when thinking about yourself and your own qualities. Because you may take wrong turns now and again, but they're *your* wrong turns, made with the best of intentions and you get to have and experience the adventures they hold. And I wouldn't trade that for anything, no matter what other people may say. Don't let people drain you: just trust yourself. And with that trust comes Peace.

57 - ARE YOU READY?

———— ❖ ————

Are you ready for your dreams to come true?

Are you ready for that job you've always wanted?

Are you ready to have children?

Are you ready to write that book?

Are you ready to ask that person out to dinner?

Are you ready for that yoga class?

Are you ready for that meditation course?

Are you ready to set up that new business?

Are you ready for that pay rise?

Of course you're not. And you never will be. But that's not the point. The point is that God/the universe/the power of love is ready for you and it always, always, always has been. And it has always, always, always been ON YOUR SIDE. Have you heard that correctly? The power of God is on your side. The power of love is working for you as your employee. The power of the entire universe and everything it contains is rooting for you and will do everything in its power to help you. So you don't have to be ready. That thought alone brings so much Peace. Allow it in and then step forward. You'll be OK.

58 - HOW'S YOUR UNIVERSE LOOKING TODAY?

❖

When you stare up at the night sky and you can see the stars and you know that we've never found the edge of space, that it could, in fact, go on forever and ever and ever and that the universe is actually expanding, so what you see is GROWING; how do you feel? Do you feel slightly overwhelmed by the sheer size of it? Or does it, perhaps, make you feel utterly tiny in comparison?

Well, the fact is that physically we are tiny. Very tiny. But if I were to tell you that the vast space you see out there is not only affected by everything you do (including your thoughts), but is also on your side throughout all of it, what would you think? Why does it matter? Because how you see the universe in relation to you and your life matters a great deal.

I don't believe that we are just inconsequential bodies that are here for a finite amount of time and then turn to dust, never to be heard of again. I believe that, as human beings, we have the entire world *and* the universe looking out for us. Willing us to know it for what it is (which is absolutely nothing but pure, unadulterated love by the way). When you think of the universe in that way it stops seeming so big and scary and instead appears to be what it is – which is our home. It is our shelter and certainly not a place that we should feel uncomfortable in. How you see the universe is directly related to how you will experience it. If you see it as foreboding because of its size, then chances are your life may have quite a bit of fear in it. If you see it as friendly, then it suddenly becomes your oyster and opens up to you, showing you its majesty and beauty. And it is beautiful. Yes, there are times when our planet acts in a way that we may not fully understand, but Nature is absolute perfection at all times unless we stick our beaks in. Then she has every right to stick up for herself. Not in a malicious or retaliatory way, but because she wants to survive also and be able to look after us.

My universe is very friendly indeed. It's like a giant cosy room in my mind and I just love being here. In fact, I'm ticked off that I may only get about 100 years tops!!

It hasn't always been this way by any means. In fact, everything outside of my bedroom used to be very scary indeed. The world was absolutely not on my side and I believed it was actively working against me. I know now that this just is not true. My view of the world and my universe was vastly different then. Nowadays I see it as home. So I feel at home. And that brings Peace. Peace on my earth.

59 - RIGHT THERE WAITING

❖

We search for those things we love, wish for and want for ourselves every day of our lives. If we're not too careful about the places and things for which we search, we'll end up looking in all the wrong places for all the wrong things. We look for jobs, titles, locations, salaries, partners, achievements, friends, possessions, holidays, trinkets, toys, fulfilment, certain feelings, escape, happiness and ultimately Peace (which is a beautifully accessible version of love).

What we are rarely, if ever, told when we are growing up is that everything we need, want or desire is already within us. Either our caretakers don't know or believe in that truth or they think that to somehow tell us this rather extraordinary secret to life will be to ruin our drive or ambition. I have noticed that I am much more 'driven' and pro-active when I am feeling encouraged and capable than when I am discouraged and feeling like I have failed so I can disprove that theory quite comfortably. But what would happen to our lives and our entire civilization, if we were told from the moment we were born that we had everything we would ever need already inside our minds, hearts and souls?

What if, no matter what our financial, social, or physical situation, those around us convinced us that we already contained the seeds to be, do, see, feel and have everything we saw in our mind's eye? How would that change our lives? How would that inform the way we think, behave and manifest the lives we've been given to live? My belief is that it would be nothing less than extraordinarily miraculous.

It would start with a thought. That thought would morph into an action. The action would become a result. The result would be Peace.

You see when you operate from a place of 'I can', not only is the journey a hell of a lot more Peaceful, but it is also a lot more loving (both to yourselves and others) because there is no sense of lack, competition or anything that doesn't resemble love in all its glory. It amazes me that we have the ability to learn to walk, talk, feel, speak and just 'be' in the first few years of our lives and then for the rest of our time here we spend it moderating those gifts instead of growing them. You are born with everything. You are absolute perfection. You are love incarnate. You were born for Peace, joy and abundance and if things should befall your path that are not of that ilk, then choose to extract all the wisdom you can from it and then get back on to your rightful path as soon as you possibly can. Because that is where your heart lies. That is where the truth of you is and that is where the truth of the entire human race is. That is where Peace is.

60 - WHO DO YOU THINK YOU ARE?

❖

Who do you think you are to even consider living that life of freedom (that you kinda know is the *right* way to live but you rarely see other people doing it)? Who do you think you are to even contemplate setting up that business? Who do you think you are holding such lofty opinions? Who do you think you are to believe that you were meant to see, do and experience more than this? Who do you think you are being this positive while those around you are hurting? Who do you think you are to believe that we're not actually here to slog our guts out in quiet desperation and then pass away? Who do you think you are to think that life could possibly work any differently for you than it does for anyone else? Who do you think you are to think that you're mentally, physically or emotionally strong enough to make a goal such as this come true?

I'll tell you who you are: You are the most perfect, precious and wonderful human being that ever walked the face of the earth. You contain within you the potential for Peace on earth. You can create joy and laughter, abundance and beauty. If you can see it in your imagination you can achieve it in your life – you are at that level of artistry.

So, I tell you to go above your station and wear your thoughts and dreams with pride, grace and laughter. Refine those fleeting pictures that flash through your mind at the oddest of moments and hold on to them for dear life, because they are visions of your futures. Every single one of you.

61 -WHEN TO CARRY THE DREAM

❖

Let me tell you what a dream worth carrying is NOT:

It is not a burden to carry.

It is not a slog or a way of life that requires force.

It is not something that will devastate you and fill you with dread in equal measures.

It is not anything that will tease you with moments of fulfilment and then long periods of silence.

Your dreams are not there to slowly drain you of life while you wait for them to materialize, and they are not there to sit in your memory as regrets.

Let me tell you what a dream worth carrying **IS**:

It is an event that you can look forward to while being able to remain totally Peaceful in the present.

It is something that may take extremely hard work to pull off but it is work that will leave you feeling spiritually and emotionally fulfilled, if a little tired physically. I call this the 'right type' of work.

It is a journey that, although you may not know the route when you start, will look out for you every step of the way. (Although hindsight is often needed to see this for the gift that it is, you should still trust it)

A dream worth carrying will call on your courage like you've never known before, but will also provide you with the Peace that goes along with it. This is the Peace that the Bible speaks of that 'passes all understanding'. You've no idea why you are able to keep going and yet you can and you do without hesitation.

It's easy to see the difference between dreams that are worth holding on to and those that are damaging to almost every aspect of your being. Dreams are extremely personal and affect us in ways that are particular to who we are and how we react to life. So sit down now with yourself and your thoughts and be ruthless. Examine the major aspects of your dreams and you'll be able to tell really quickly how they make you feel. Don't think I don't acknowledge that this could possibly be one of the hard-est and most brutal things you'll do with your life. Many of us carry around dreams that are not dreams at all. They are simply ideas mixed in with a whole heap of expecta-tions and, over time, they end up not being our dreams at all as they don't fit into the dreams that the person we have become would hold. So I'd like to offer you the most incredible way to get your destiny back on the right track and get your heart, soul and mind back on the path to Peace. If you're getting the sense that the dreams you've been hanging on to are not the right ones for you, then I urge you to let them go. This will be pretty scary and you may even have a time when you have to grieve the loss of the life that you thought you might yet get to live. But I promise you, although hard, something magical happens when we let something go for all the right reasons. Our dreams are allowed to morph into what they truly should be and then they come back to us in complete perfection. But you have to let it go fully. No hanging on to a part of it that's working. You have to create a pure vacuum that can then be filled by the power of the deep love that works in our lives when we only step back and let it.

This is a win–win situation, I absolutely promise you. And one of the most remarkable things that happens the moment we let go of something that is not quite right, is that Peace descends on us. It envelops us in its goodness and clarity and never, ever leaves us. Unless we poke our nose where it shouldn't be. So let go, receive the Peace that is your birthright and watch your *real* dreams unfold in front of your eyes.

62 - HOW IS FEAR CREATED?

————— ❖ —————

Something that I had to get to grips with in my own life was that if I was lacking Peace, it was my responsibility to get it back. I found it very easy to lay the blame for my circumstances at other people's feet. Especially when it seemed pretty clear to me that I had done nothing wrong. That's the real kicker: when we are seemingly blameless and yet still our whole situation seems to fall apart. Then it's incredibly easy to shift blame and the lack of Peace in our lives on to the perpetrator. Even so, perhaps distressingly, it is still our responsibility to get our own Peace back. But it's that simple acknowledgement of responsibility that takes us immediately on to the path back to gaining Peace. I can assure you that this isn't a trick to make us more independent of others and immune to hurt. Instead, this is the calmest and most fulfilling, loving and joy inducing way to get Peace back into our lives after a blow has been dealt to hurt us. Yes, within our unfamiliarity of the power of this situation to potentially transform our lives, the fact that we have to do the work and the forgiving to get the Peace back that has been stolen from us seems a touch unfair. But that is a myth. Nothing at all has been stolen from us and nothing that we hold within us can be stolen. And the amount that we hold within us is phenomenal and rarely looked at in its entirety.

It's not possible for another person to steal our Peace unless *we* let them. It is not possible for another person to cause us to permanently lose our confidence unless *we* let it go. I railed against this in pure indignation for such a long time. The sheer unfairness of it was utterly baffling to me, but Peace continued to stay at arms' length from my life the longer I held on to that burning rock of blame. And, the longer I held on to it, the more of a negative impact it had on my life.

Fear is created in us, by us. It is only *triggered* by events and circumstances and only we can remove it from our lives. We have to sit down with fear, look it dead in the eye and explain to it that its company is not welcome in any way, shape or form in our life. We need to tell it that we have chosen another direction and won't be pulled off that path. That act allows Peace to enter.

63 - ABUNDANCE IS A FEELING

❖

I absolutely love the concept of 'abundance'. I love the word, the way it sounds and, most importantly, I love the way the word makes me feel. Abundance to me is looking at what I have and being grateful for it, as opposed to looking at what I don't have and feeling dissatisfied. These days I find it a great deal easier to tap in to the feeling of abundance. I have practised doing it and over time I have become better at it.

It wasn't always this way. Abundance was an alien concept to me and not something that I believed I could partake of or experience for any length of time. The word 'abundance' was one that rarely, if ever passed my lips and the sheer possibility of it scared me somewhat in as much as I feared losing it should it ever pass my way. Isn't it odd that I should push something as delicious as abundance away before it even had a chance to reach me?

When we speak of abundance we often think in terms of things, objects and money. And this is correct to a point because money can buy stuff and accumulating lots of things can make us see our lives as abundant. But although we can experience abundance through physical objects, I believe that abundance is actually a feeling that can manifest itself in us when we allow it to and in spite of what our material situation looks like. So surely that begs the question that if we were to feel abundant on a daily basis, no matter what our circumstances, we would BE abundant? I mean, who could possibly tell us otherwise if that is the way we felt?

What we need to know is how to create a feeling of abundance when we often look around and see nothing but what we lack, who is in pain and what it is about our life that hurts. And therein lies the problem. In *noticing* those things that cause us to feel less than abundant we prolong and enlarge our perceived situation. Yet in noticing and celebrating what we have right now we can also prolong and enlarge that perceived situation. I may look at you and all that you have around you and find it baffling that you don't think you're the richest person who ever lived, but my opinion isn't really going to help you a bit. On the other hand, I may look at the way your life has gone and feel pity for you and the way it turned out, but if you are living your life with an intense feeling of abundance within your mind, heart and soul then who the heck am I to question that? In those cases I know nothing about you. But you? You know everything. You know how to turn the light of abundance on in your life simply by flicking the switch from noticing what you don't have to noticing what you do. I've seen this work in so many people's lives and it's reached the point where I'm now really aware of who is operating from a feeling of abundance and who isn't. And let me tell you, it is not always to do with stuff, possessions, money or things. Abundance transcends all of that and if we inhabit a spirit of abundance, it pours like precious oil through our veins and seeps out of our pores as a life that is full to the brim with love, Peace and joy. That is abundance, it is a feeling, and it brings Peace with it.

64 - ALLOW IT TO MAKE YOU FEEL GOOD

❖

Even the most beautiful pictures and inspiring quotes can fill us with discontent or feelings of inadequacy when it's not our 'real' self that's viewing them. Our real selves know that those beautiful pictures are no reflection on us personally; that they are simply a snapshot of what the world around us is capable of being. So let me say something to you if you don't feel that your world matches up to what you see out there: your life can be as beautiful, as big, as bold and as bountiful as you'd like it to be, no matter what stage it's at right *now*. You can, and I know you will, put one foot in front of the other and move forward with your life, no matter where you're starting from. And if you see pictures of the world or places and people that make you feel like you're lacking, but secretly you know that deep down that's because you yearn to experience those things yourself, then it's absolutely vital that you open yourself up to that beauty instead of pushing it away.

If your mantra is 'There is no Lack', then everything that

you see around you will inspire you to greatness and not drag you down to feelings of inadequacy. There is enough of everything to go around I assure you. We simply have to refine our feel-good receptors. Firstly, we have to know what to let in and what not to. And secondly, we have to learn to detect within ourselves why it is that we feel certain ways when we see certain things.

Seeing an image of something we dearly want can be extremely painful. I understand that a great deal as I found it hard to see images of anything to do with babies when I was struggling with getting, and staying, pregnant. But there is a path you can take through imagery that will lead you on to the most delicious journey of fulfillment that you could possibly imagine. When we see images of things we love that actually exist in the world, that's all the proof we need that they could exist in our lives too. Why should something be for one person and not another. THERE IS NO LACK! This understanding only comes after we've shed our cloak of envy of those things that are not yet ours. But when we do we'll realize just how much inspiration is out there for us to add to our lives. And not only is that where the fun begins, but it is also a place of great Peace.

65 - IT NEVER SHOULD HAVE BEEN THIS WAY

❖

'It never should have been this way.' 'My life should never have turned out like this.' Really? Well there's two things that I think need to be discussed here:

1. You are in control of a great deal more of your life than you think.
2. You are in absolute control of how you react and respond to those things that happen in your life.

I went through a period when I seemed to lose everything that I'd worked for. Relationships, money, reputation, confidence – you name it, it was going down the drain. I looked at my life and could not understand why this was happening. I'd been given more opportunities than most people get in a lifetime and yet I still couldn't make it work. I was the person who was saying to anyone who would listen: 'It never should have been this way', when what I needed to be saying to myself was: 'So what am I going to do about it?'

Hindsight, when it relates to us personally, can be excruciating because we are likely to spot the mistakes we have made and then want to kick ourselves for making them. But, if we can be brutally honest with ourselves when going through this process we can boil these painful 'WHY ME?!' moments in our lives down to the two points I have just mentioned. Then, perhaps, our stream of consciousness can go something like this instead: *'OK, sure, I made some really bad choices and I know better now so I'll not make them again. But I'm not getting angry with myself or anyone else for that matter. I have experienced the power of forgiveness before and it is thoroughly underrated. So I forgive myself, everyone else involved and CHOOSE to move forward in lightness.'*

Unforgiveness, in any guise, is a lead weight to carry around with you and, over time, you realize that the strain it has on your heart, mind and soul can be irreparable if left unchecked. But what interests me the most about this powerful process is what happens after we've chosen to forgive. It seems like a veil is being lifted and we begin to see the situation we've just escaped in a very different light and, invariably, as time goes on, we'll find that we actually end up being grateful for what went before because we wouldn't be where we are now without it. I know I wouldn't be here writing this book had it not been for certain episodes in my life. Some I could have avoided; some I could not, but in all of them I had a choice as to how I would react and that's what I bring to my life now. The experience, the knowledge, the wisdom, the Peace. Ahhhhh, the Peace.

66 - MORE, MORE, MORE

❖

Ok, the moment you feel like you need to put a halt on all the fabulous dreams, ambitions and plans for your life remember this one thing - The more you have, the more you can give away. And giving away to others is one of the biggest buzzes you can have in life. It is the ultimate natural high. So be greedy for the good stuff. Allow it to pour out on to your life like the deliciousness of soft butter melting on to creamy mashed potato. And then pass it around because, let's be honest, who can resist creamy mashed potato?!

67 - THERE IS NO LACK

❖

No matter how much you acquire in life, if you've acquired it through the right intentions, it is impossible to deny anyone anything. There is always enough if we attract the things that are meant for us and we do that by being in alignment and having the right intention. Easier said than done, yes – and yet it is possible.

You'll find that as you move through life and hone your practice of living in alignment and behaving with the right intentions, your life will become rather full. Almost by accident and almost without you realizing why, the material possessions that you lusted after for so long and always seemed a hair's breadth out of reach will suddenly just appear and you'll probably have no idea how they got there. Not that you'll mind them being there, you'll LOVE having them. You'll also LOVE giving some of them away because, as you'll discover, that's where the real buzz is. And there will be one thing missing from the feeling that accompanies this material bounty: the fear of losing it all.

You see, when all this material possession stuff happens, you'll not really notice it because you'll have been really busy. Busy growing emotionally and spiritually. Busy practising living in alignment and having the purest intentions imaginable.

You'll have noticed quite by chance that us human beings have been underestimated for too long and we're actually really bloody powerful when it comes to getting things done. But only if alignment and intention are in the right places. You'll be able to handle the money, the possessions, the luxury, the responsibility and the organization that goes along with that sort of lifestyle because you'll have done all the inner work needed. Because alignment and intention are in the right places and they lead only to Peace.

68 - I'M A BELIEVER

❖

Know in your soul that you'll get there. It doesn't matter where 'there' is, but know deep in your self that you'll make it. That you will arrive at a place of Peace in your life and that you'll stay there. There may be other challenges after the one you're currently facing but know in your soul that you'll get there with those, too. Carry this knowledge around with you every single moment of every single day. This knowledge is Peace personified and will serve you faithfully on your journey through life.

69 - YOU CAN DO IT BECAUSE YOU ARE DOING IT

❖

How often, in the midst of doing something, have you stopped and thought to yourself: 'I can't do this'? More times than you can count, I'm sure. I do it all the time. But one day, when I was deep into the act of doing something and the thought struck me, for the first time I saw just how illogical telling myself that really was. If you are, in fact, in the middle of doing something then it's impossible for you NOT to be able to do it, surely? If you can do it, then you can't suddenly *not* do it? Remember this when doubt comes knocking. Remember it when you have a wobble. Remember it when you're criticized. Remember this when it doesn't go as well as you'd hoped.

You can do it because you ARE doing it. And within that knowledge lies Peace.

70 - THE POWER OF
PERCEPTION

❖

There was a time, when my children were even smaller than they are now, that seemed monumentally tough. I felt detached from life for almost a year, or so it seemed, and Peace in my life was absolutely nowhere to be found. During that time, I took a great many pictures on my iPhone and at the end of the year, using an app that I had downloaded, I put together a compilation of my favourite pictures and set this slideshow to music. The first thing I noticed was that I was struggling to pick the right amount of pictures for the purpose of this slideshow. I had far too many that I wanted to use and so had to cut a lot of them. So judging by that the year couldn't have been that awful, right? I mean if it had been horrific I wouldn't want to see a single image from that time. I set the slideshow to the music of Einaudi and felt absolutely distraught when I watched it back that I had carried such a different view of the year from the one that was presented to me in these clips. In the clips that I was seeing, that I had taken with my own hand, there was life and beauty, soul and joy. In my mind, there was loneliness and struggle in the year that I found really hard.

Which image was the truth? The truth is, in fact, whatever I want it to be. It could be the year of slog or the year of joy and upon seeing a year presented to me in such a joyful way, I chose to see that year as one of the best in my life. Because suddenly it WAS!!! So, by viewing those events in a different way I managed to completely obliterate a shitty year in my mind. Nowadays, I actually couldn't tell you what it was about that year that I struggled with without having to think hard and remember. But I could tell you all the good bits.

I find it irritating when people and the media criticize ordinary people using social media to make their lives look better. I don't want to get into semantics here, as I know what your response will be if you are one of those people. Instead, I say GO FORTH and make your life as beautiful as you possibly can and then SHOUT about it from the rooftops. Put beautiful pictures of the life you love on to whatever platform you want to. I wish that my mum had had Instagram when I was growing up as I'd love to see what she would have posted. Tell us all about the progress you're making at work or how your garden is coming along. Use whatever filter you like to make it look better because in the end, does it really matter? No. What really matters is that we're investing in our lives and creating the lives we want to live. We're not just sitting back and settling for bad memories and a false perception of what we think things were like.

I've never taken time for granted in the same way again since I got the shock of seeing a whole year in pictures. If only I'd have known that my perception of that time was all off perhaps I could have been more present. I still have the pictures of that time and that is a blessing but I'll not allow myself to be robbed of the experience again. There was Peace in that year. I just had to look for it.

71 - BORN WITH EVERYTHING

❖

Apart from obvious things like the ability to walk and talk, we are born with everything we need to lead a Peace-full life and a life full of Peace (two separate things, when you think about it). When we are born:

- We have a pure heart that knows only love and how to love
- We have the right intentions
- We are born in alignment
- We have no fear
- We know nothing of judgement or prejudice

There are many more qualities that we come in to this world carrying, but just those five would see you living a life that is abundant in Peace. What is sad is that when we realize this, we spend a great deal of our adult lives trying to reset our factory settings. We actually want to go back to the creation we were when we first came in to the world. The innocent, unsullied, friendly, Peace-full being that feels so damn good to us.

But the good news is that we don't have to *try* to do that. This state is already in us. It *is* us. We just need to remember it. We just need to *be* it.

72 - ACHIEVING PEACE THROUGH LAUGHTER

❖

To have fun is to be at Peace. Try it. It doesn't matter what type of fun you have; just do whatever makes you laugh so hard your sides hurt. Laugh so much that you wipe the tears away from your eyes and feel ever so slightly exhausted by it. Then start laughing again. Laugh until no sound comes out and you're just sat there with your eyes clenched shut and your mouth wide open. You'll still be laughing, the effects will still be the same, and you'll know Peace then.

Peace isn't always quiet and serene. Peace can be raucous, giggly, loud, honest, and mischievous. And it can also be (my absolute favorite) irreverent. If someone is unashamedly irreverent, then they have my heart forever. Peace comes in so many forms and I wanted to dedicate a whole chapter to the fact that Peace is exciting as well as calming. It is fun as well as faithful and it is a force to be reckoned with. It is very hard to sink, or even shake, a ship that sails in constant Peace. And when you have a ship sailing in Peace, while also having fun, wow, now *that* is a journey I'd like to take.

73 - THE PEACE IN ALLOWING

❖

Take a look at what is happening in your life right now. How does it make you feel? Safe? Cosy? Alert? Creative? Loving? Uncomfortable? Panicky? Fearful? Agitated? Sometimes, and only sometimes, it's really important to sit with and allow whatever you are feeling just to be there for a while before acting upon it. And there are two ways in which this can be done:

1. If the circumstances of your life are pretty positive right now, then sit there with those warm and healing feelings that arise from them and actually allow your body to feel them in the most physical way that you can. By doing this, you banish the fear of those great times not lasting by creating a muscle memory in your body that will enable you to recreate great feelings when times are tougher. And it's very possible for good times and great emotions to be physically felt by your body. In me, they manifest as Peace. Pure and simple Peace and

I've trained my body to reconnect to that feeling at will because I believe that is the natural state humans should be in. At Peace.

2. When your feelings are less than positive and you want nothing more than to get rid of them, this is how I believe you can find Peace again. Sit with the feelings you have, do not instil them with any more energy or feelings as they have enough already. Sit with them dispassionately and *without* fear. Allow them to be in the room with you without touching you emotionally. It is at this time that you will be able to leave that place and move forward to create anew without dragging any of the negativity with you. But without doing this you will end up carrying these hard feelings around like unwanted hitchhikers. They're in your car but you're going at such great speed that it's impossible to let them out.

Believe me, it's just as hard to allow the great feelings in as it is to disallow the horrid ones. But it's possible if your motivation is Peace. And I can assure you that once you have experienced Peace, you'll need no other motivation.

74 - HOW FAR WILL YOU GO?

❖

Our lives are in constant motion. Everything around us moves all the time. When we're asleep, our heart keeps moving the blood around our body. When we touch something that seems solid the atoms within it move as it's full of much more space than we'll ever see with the naked eye. That's why when you come up against challenges, difficulties or loss in your life, don't think for one moment that the world has stopped moving because it hasn't. The world will never stop moving, the universe may never stop growing and your current situation won't feel like this forever. It is impossible for our lives to stop unless we actively halt them. Even then, they'll not stop, but they won't flourish either. They may wither if we decide to put a halt to our lives. We've all seen people who have done that to themselves, to their lives and even to the lives of others because of an event that they find impossible to 'move on' from.

Your life will take you as far as your thoughts and feelings allow it to. Don't put a halt on your life because you're currently up against it. Allow it to move on from this point and into Peace and it shall. It's impossible for it not to if you choose to allow it.

75 - BEING BUSY. CHOOSING A DIFFERENT BRAND

❖

I used to view busy people as so lucky! They must be so accomplished to have all that going on in their lives. And I strived to join them, to be busy, to be a part of the gang. I equated being busy with value, and yet, as I steadily became busier, I realized that the value that I was adding to any aspect of my life was decreasing exponentially. I mistook busyness for effectiveness, and recognizing and acknowledging that fact was one of the best things I ever could have done, not only for my own productivity, but, more importantly, for Peace in my life.

Most people have bought into the brand of 'Busyness', just as I did. But the defining characteristics of busyness and effectiveness are that busyness, over time, will break you, while you, in reality, don't get nearly as much done as you could. Whereas, effectiveness will enhance your life beyond measure, while enabling you to get everything you want done. And with that knowledge comes Peace – as anyone with a *full* life will tell you.

So, ask yourself today: am I busy or am I effective? Effectiveness will enhance how you get things done while you simultaneously change the world. That's a pretty good trade I'd say.

76 - THE DANGER OF DISTRACTION

❖

There are a great many things that can distract us during our day and I've read countless articles on how to be more productive and get more done in less time, etc. But when we have so many distracters in many different forms - things like email, text messages, social media, constant news cycles, the internet, a million TV channels and opinions all over the place being written by folk who know next to nothing, then we have to be able to add a filter of our own that works very well. If you feel like you're not quite hitting the nail on the head in the progress you make day to day, then ask yourself this one question – and asking it will be the only filter you need since the way you answer it will determine your direction: *'Is what I am doing right now helping me to fulfill my destiny as the person I was put on this earth to be?'* When you answer that question, remember that each time a second, minute, hour or day passes, you are not going to get them back. I don't remind you of this to panic you but rather to highlight that each and every moment you spend here is utterly precious with regards to who you are as a human being. And when we're operating from a place of deep alignment with regards to who we are and what we truly believe we are here to achieve it will bring us Peace.

Only *you* have *yourself* to offer the world, so don't get distracted from offering it the *best* of you at all times.

77 - WHEN YOU GIVE AWAY YOUR POWER YOU GIVE AWAY YOUR PEACE

❖

My background is in theatre and acting. I was lucky enough to study at the Royal Central School of Speech and Drama, one of the most prestigious drama schools in the world and had experiences that I will never forget. The teaching staff were second to none and the standard of acting that they managed to get out of each and every one of us by our third year was remarkable. For the first two years of study, we didn't come into any contact with agents or casting directors, and we were rather cocooned, but that all changed the day we started back for our third year.

Acting was the stuff of dreams for me at that time. It was interesting, fun, creative and fulfilling. But in year three, we had to change our thinking slightly as suddenly, we were all competing with each other. The classmates who I'd spent time studying the most wonderful subjects, stories and characters with were now, almost overnight, going for exactly the same meetings with the same agents and then on to the same auditions for the same parts with the same casting directors. Now it was real life and the womb-like existence of drama school had come to an end. I had to face classmates on the steps outside the school when I'd been successful in securing an agent and they hadn't. I had to congratulate a classmate when he or she had won a part in a huge new production that I had also auditioned for. I saw some of my fellow students' careers as likely to 'take off', while sometimes it felt like mine was likely to falter.

If I could go back in time and meet myself as I stood on those steps outside drama school, this is what I would tell myself: 'The parts you audition for, the agents and the casting directors don't have a bearing on your destiny. I know it doesn't seem like that right now but your confidence in yourself is a much greater fulfiller of dreams than those external people are. Don't give other people power over your life; it's not yours to give away. Your life is to be lived in joy, abundance and Peace and if you give it to someone else they will not know what to do with it. Giving your power, and therefore your Peace, will not benefit you (the giver) or them (the receiver). Keep in the front of your mind that there is no lack of anything in the world, ever. And if you don't happen to be right for one part then there is another that is better.'

I am pretty certain that most dreams and visions for our lives would lead us to believe that dependence on other, more powerful people is a pre-requisite for success. Well it's not. It's helpful, undoubtedly, but you also need to have a rock solid sense of self that will withstand any fall or rejection along the way. Hold on to your power, don't give it away to people it doesn't belong to, and keep your own faith. Then you'll have a Peace-full journey to your destiny.

78 - A GIFT WRAPPED AS GRIEF

❖

In the space of four years, between 2009 and 2014, I learnt the meaning of the words loss, fear and grief. But also during that time I had two beautiful children come into the world, my husband recovered from cancer and my first three books were published. I also had great times with friends, made memories with my family that will last forever and saw more miracles take place than I can possibly count. I lived in beautiful homes for varying amounts of time and I met and worked with some amazing people.

But, and I feel wretched for saying this even now, for a great deal of that time the stress of the bad far outweighed the miraculous and the love of the positive – until, that is, one moment on my sofa when I had what can only be described as a miraculous moment. For just a second I felt at Peace. I can only describe it as a wave of Peace that travelled across my mind and my body and for just a moment I felt totally different from how I'd been feeling for so long. I guess I must have been feeling so bad that to feel good was an absolute shock to my system and designed so that I would NEVER miss it. I felt Peace-full and I knew in that instant that in actual fact this was how my life (and all of our lives) were meant to feel *all* of the time. It was a gift of pure grace that I experienced this and I don't know where I would be had it not happened. But it did and I never want to be without it again. That much I know.

So I now have the ability to look upon the times of struggle and the residue of damage that they left imprinted on my mind as a gift. A gift wrapped up in loss, fear, stress and grief, but a gift all the same. An invaluable gift that allows me to write this book about a subject I feel so passionately about and have to share with others as if my life depended on it. My life, the one I believe I'm born to live, does depend on Peace and I love it.

79 - THE POWER OF LIGHT

❖

Let me give you an incredibly powerful image to use when you feel that the darkness in your life is all consuming and you're not strong enough to fight it off.

You're sitting in a darkened cinema. The lights have gone down and the film is yet to start, so you are in complete darkness. Right over the other side of the cinema, in the farthest possible seat from you someone lights a cigarette with a match. You can see the flame from the match immediately. You may even be able to see the hand that lights the cigarette, the cigarette itself and the face of the person lighting that cigarette. *THAT* is how powerful one small bit of light can be. It can cut through a room filled with black with only one flame and totally destroy complete darkness is an instant. Fear is that dark room. Love, courage, forgiveness, joy and Peace is that flame.

80 - DOES IT MATTER? REALLY?

❖

Does it matter that they said that? Really? Does it matter that you felt that way? Really? Does it matter that you were passed over? Really?

Does it matter that you were ignored? Really? They didn't invite you. Does it matter? Really? Their intentions were not the same as yours. You know that now. Does it matter? Really? You thought you were friends. They didn't. Does it matter? Really?

What I'm trying to do in this chapter is really to ask you to take a look at what you are expending your precious thoughts, time and energy on. Because if it's on things, people, events, situations or feelings that really do not matter to the growth, Peace, joy and abundance in your life then I would say, without a moment's hesitation, that you are wasting huge swathes of your life with this type of worrying and perhaps ruining your health as well. Because, and this is one of the most freeing things you'll ever know (literally, your life will change) – when you remove your own ego from each one of these situations very few, if any, things are worth worrying about.

Find the difference between what you should and should not allow into your heart, head and mind and stick to that. My guess is that once you've let go of the small-minded/ego-based thoughts that used to rule your emotions, you'll turn to things that are far larger and much more satisfying. In this larger space you will find Peace. You'll also find a great deal more fun, excitement and joy, but Peace will be there in abundance.

81 - FINDING THE PEACE IN PRAISE

❖

What do you do when someone pays you a compliment? Especially when it's on or about something that you're not very confident? How do you respond? How do you feel? What do you say? Think? Do? Do you deflect the compliment and respond by totally denying that it was anything to do with you and all the work of other people? Do you brush it off like it really isn't worth even commenting on? Do you slather on that old self-deprecation so thickly that no one in his or her right mind would even bother to penetrate it? Or do you say, 'Awww, thanks so much, it was so much fun to be involved', or perhaps, 'well, yes, I've been on a bit of a health kick lately and I have to say I'm feeling absolutely brilliant.'

If you're in the second group of people and can find the Peace in accepting praise for the things you have done, then you will know greater happiness, I promise you. Deflecting praise or compliments is thoroughly unnecessary and utterly ridiculous. It leaves you feeling robbed of an acknowledgement that you should have and also leaves the other person feeling miffed that he or she even bothered. And that's not a recipe for Peace. I cannot say this loud enough – you are not being egotistical by accepting a compliment. You are being emotionally mature; you clearly know your worth as a human being, and you know that compliments, just like love, make the world go round. They are the icing on the cake, the sun in the sky and the hug, which whether we know it or not, we need. Accept them and pass them on. Then you are in your own small way spreading Peace around the globe.

82 - WHAT LIES BEYOND THIS DIFFICULT TIME?

❖

If there's one thing I wish I could give you it would be the ability to see beyond your current situation to what lies on the other side of it. I know that would require a time machine of sorts, but if there's one thing I want to reassure you of it's that Peace lies on the other side of what you're currently going through. I promise. *But* it is entirely up to you how long it takes you to reach it.

The fact is we can stay where we are for as long as we like. Days, weeks, months, years. I've even known people to stay in one place emotionally for their entire lives. But I've also encountered people who have made the choice to pull back the curtain and dare to look at what's on the other side. They've dared to believe that this, too, shall pass and they've dared to accept that it's up to them as to how long it'll take. I truly understand that it's immensely difficult when you don't know how to begin to hope that the situation you find yourself in will change for the better one day. But if all you are able to do is to say to yourself at the start of each day, 'I am here to live in abundance, Peace and joy' and use that as your motivation across all aspects of your life and behaviours, I cannot describe to you how quickly your situation will change. Peace lies beyond your current tough situation, that is true, and you have everything you need to be able to travel towards it. Only you can determine how long your journey will take.

83 - IN SEARCH OF PEACE

❖

When people have a deep sense of Peace it can cause quite a reaction in those who do not. Seeing someone else at Peace can be one of the most painful things that a person in distress can witness (I know this because it caused pain in me when I saw it). It's so jarring that it's almost hard to comprehend. We often call this jealousy, insecurity or a lack of love for oneself, but I believe that these emotions are just symptoms of a lack of Peace in that person's life. Having Peace gives you a sense of happiness, confidence and a calmness that shines from inside of you. It's not something that people who are at Peace in themselves can manufacture; it's just there, in them, and is very powerful to observers, even though it's hard to articulate what it is that's different about them.

If you wish for Peace in your life then I urge you to seek out Peace-full people. If you don't know of any right now then just put the request 'out there', believe that they will cross your path and when you find one make it your business to get to know them. Learn from them, ask if there's anything you can do to help them so that you are able to spend time in their company. See how they interact with other people and ask them questions. Observe them and take notes on how they live, how they behave, what sorts of things bother them and what things they simply let go of. Seek Peace out in people, learn from them and begin to install Peace in your own life. What you'll find is that, once you attract one Peace-full person in to your life, you'll start to notice that there are, in fact, a great many more out there waiting for you to know and learn from. They'll just appear. The Law of Attraction is very strong so use it wisely.

To consciously attract Peace-full people into your life is, and I'm not exaggerating, life-changing. So before you make a decision to do it write down the date and how you feel on the day you begin and keep it safe. Then go back to this list a year later and staring up at you will be proof of a miraculous change in your life. I'd love to hear about it so please feel free to email me at cherry@cherrymenlove. com because if there's one type of email I love to receive it's the tale of a miracle in someone's life.

84 - CREATE IN PEACE, NOT PAIN

❖

I believe that we're all creative in our own ways. No one type of person has the monopoly on creativity, and yet it can seem like that when different personalities get together and one is perhaps louder or more vocal about their creativity than another. The writer, the artist, the musician, the actor, and so on, all appear to be 'more' creative than the accountant perhaps, but that doesn't have to be true. I married an accountant and I find that the way he thinks about process, strategy and the bigger picture is very creative and is something that I (as the writer) could never do.

One aspect of creativity in one's working life that bothers me more than most others is the image of the tortured artist. When I see someone creating for a living and that work bringing them nothing but pain and that they seem to rely on that pain to make the work, I think that's a bit topsy turvy. Creativity is meant to breathe life into us. It is meant to be healing, not just to us, but also to the other people who view, see, hear or listen to it. Yes, it is absolutely vital that we portray the darker side of life or even our own lives, and we have to communicate with authenticity or it'll fall flat. And yes, sometimes that authenticity will have to reveal that the story doesn't always end well. I understand all of that. Yet, I still believe that the image of a 'mantle' that the tortured artist has to wear to do good work should be actively discouraged. Why? Because I believe we are able to do better work when we are at Peace. When we can look back at the darker times of our life through the eyes of healing and Peace, we still have the ability to communicate raw emotion. And I truly believe that we'll have the ability to portray those feelings, or that time, with *more* depth than if we insist on staying in that moment and in that pain, because we're an 'artist'. We're not going to lose our creative edge if we're happy, but we will lose our ego, and the ego always, without fail, impacts negatively on what we are trying to create. Find Peace in your life as a creative person. Destroy the cliché and change the world. It's not only about you; it's about the people who you can possibly change forever for the better through your actions and work.

85 - SURRENDER

❖

I f you are new to Peace, you'll find that, as you get further down the road with this new travelling companion occasionally things will start to feel a little uncomfortable. This is fine and it's to be expected. Hooking up with Peace and having it in your life is a little like falling in love (except with Peace the romance stays around forever instead of diminishing, that's how wonderful it is). But when we first fall in love there's often a time when we are so happy and things are going so well, we can almost think that the bottom may fall out because 'nothing can possibly be this perfect'. If you start to feel like that it's fine, don't panic. But for goodness' sake don't shut yourself off from Peace either. It's not the fault of Peace and it's not your fault either. It's as simple as you just not being *used* to having Peace in your life for any sustained length of time. It can feel a bit like winning the lottery. Where's the worry gone? Where's the insecurity and erratic thoughts about things that may or not happen? Where are the tummy pains and the headaches? Even the arguments have disappeared from life and your social circle has grown, what's up with that! And hey, look at that! Your business has never done this well; you can take a holiday!!

These events and feelings that come with Peace can bring up all sorts of emotions, namely fear, but please remember that fear does not have to contain any power – and it's up to you whether you allow it to even exist in your life. Surrender to Peace, instead. It's like a hot bath, a dip in a tranquil ocean or watching the sunset in the most beautiful place on earth. It will serve you very well and transform all aspects of your life, but only if you let it in. Push out the fear, let in the Peace.

86 - FRAUDSTER

❖

Who are you to think that you can write this book?

Who are you to think that you can set this business up?

Who are you to think that you can be fulfilled in what you do?

Who are you to think that you can parent?

Who are you to believe that you can make it out of poverty and live a life of comfort?

Who are you to believe that you can put the past behind you and move forward in strength?

Who are you to think that anyone ever gets over abuse?

Who are you to believe that you'll be one of the very few to make it as a reformed drug user when so many others have failed?

Who are you to show your face after what we've seen about you on the internet?

Who are you to think that you can leave this town and make it on your own?

Who are you? You're a fraud if you think you can do any of these things.

Recognize any of these thoughts? I'm sure most of us have had at least two or three of those in our lives. So what's the answer? Who are you? You're utterly and absolutely perfectly YOU. There is not another you on this planet and that is what makes you qualified to carry out every dream, ambition, healing or journey that you ever want to undertake. You are a human being so start '*BE-ING*' right now. Be love. Be confidence. Be Peace-full. Be aspirational. Be strong. Be beautiful. Be funny. Be healthy. Be transformed. Be spiritual. Be hardworking. Be wise. Be humble. Be social. Be friends with a million people. Love a billion people.

Be. At. Peace.

87 - MAKE PEACE WITH YOUR PATH

❖

Your life's path is going to be full of twists and turns. You'll be walking down a sweetly scented lane one day and thrown into brambles among the thorns the next. But here's something we can learn from a group of people I admire – explorers.

You see, if you're an explorer, you never set off on an exploratory trip without preparing as much as you can before you leave. Explorers never know exactly what they are going to come across or face, but they prepare as best they can before they even pack their bags. We need to be teaching our children that this is one of the most valuable life skills one can have: to prepare for the path our life will take, even though we don't know it, and decide to live it and walk it in Peace before we even set off. When you are 'at Peace' or Peace-Full with yourself and your situation, then whatever may be thrown at your feet, you'll find it easier to cope with. But if your life is just a series of lurches to the left and right, with no equilibrium whatsoever, and drama at every turn, you will never reach your full potential. Too much energy is being used just keeping you from going absolutely nuts, let alone from fulfilling your purpose.

Let me tell you a secret: what you *think* matters right now doesn't matter one bit. I'll tell you what matters – PEACE working, living and influencing your life, your behavior and, therefore, your dreams. Choose your path. Choose Peace. And, thereby, choose Life.

88 - DECIDE UPON WHAT YOU WILL ALLOW IN

❖

To change our lives, our environment, our minds, our hearts and our destinies we have to start seeing the world differently. A WHOLE lot differently. I'm not going to lie to you; this will be hard to do. We are constantly surrounded by other people's (and the media's) way of looking at the world and it seeps into our consciousness without us even realizing. And, if what is seeping in is negative then we're at the mercy of what other people want us to know about.

The older I get, the more I believe that to really thrive in this world I can't just focus on the things I hear or read about in the news. I know what is going on and some of it is so horrific and heartbreaking to me that I struggle to make it through a whole article or segment. But there is also a very large part of me that knows that the goodness in this life far, FAR, outweighs the badness. So I raise my thought level off of what I've just seen or heard and move it on to a far higher level of Peace, goodness, consciousness and love. I do that because I believe that when I am there I can really help make a difference. But I can do no good and make no positive difference if my thinking is calibrated at the same level as the issues that are so heartbreaking. I'm not talking about living some kind of monk-like existence or denying that there are things that happen that need to change, but I am acutely aware of the fact that if you meet negativity with more negativity you get negativity. And that's the same with all discordant issues.

This principle is exactly the same one that runs through all the major religions and philosophies around the world so that is not a new concept to us. It's: *Karma, Reaping what you sow; Do as you would be done by; The law of attraction; You become what you think about.*

If we meet these situations with calmness, Peace, wisdom, a clear idea of what is right, wrong and tolerable then we'll have an extraordinarily different experience of many of the issues we face today. And we'll end up with Peace.

89 - COMPARE AT YOUR PERIL

❖

Have you ever witnessed someone who you love, adore and think is wonderful comparing him or herself to somebody else in a negative way? I have, often, and it breaks my heart. The effects of comparison are numerous and extremely damaging. You'll just have to take my word for it on this, but if you don't believe me, try to stop and think about how you feel the moment you start comparing yourself negatively to another person. Wretched, no doubt. Absolutely wretched. I'm all for other people inspiring us to achieve our own destinies, but when we compare ourselves to others, we're comparing ourselves to *THEIR* destinies and that is sheer lunacy. There is no lack of people on the planet, so there is no lack of adventures to be had or destinies to be fulfilled.

I'm going to use 'Stop, Look and Listen', a little road safety slogan from my childhood in the mid-70s to illustrate my point.

Stop – when you see something you love, want or aspire to just stop.

Look – of course you must look – how can we know what we want in our life if we don't look at it.

Listen – listen to yourself. What are you saying the moment you see the thing, person or environment you most aspire to be or dream of? If it's anything other than 'that is absolutely beautiful, I would love to experience that' then don't say it. There can never be thoughts that run through your head that go something like 'I *wish* I was … blah, blah, blah'. If you *wish* for anything it ain't never going to happen. We are not here to wish for anything because there is no lack. We are here to *live* in joy, Peace and abundance, and comparing yourself to another person has absolutely nothing to do with that. It doesn't matter if you both do the same job and the person you are comparing yourself to is making millions at it a year and you're making £notsomuch. Only YOU can do the job, or any job, the way *you* would do it.

Find *your* strength and believe in yourself. You are unique and in the realization of your own uniqueness will lie your Peace. With that Peace you will soar.

90 - THE PEACE TO PROSPER

❖

God forbid you do too well in life, eh? Gracious, if you get more of ANYTHING than the next person, you'll obviously change beyond recognition and become one of 'them'. We've all heard it: 'She thinks she's so 'calm' since she started doing yoga.' [Sneer.] 'He's no fun since he began losing all the weight.' 'Have you seen what that promotion has done to her? Bleugh.' 'I hear his new venture is doing well. One day he'll be sorry he left the security of his job when it fails.' 'They meditate a lot. So basically they sit around on the floor doing nothing but humming.' 'She *seems* really happy. Makes my skin crawl. No one is that happy.'

The question is – who would you rather be? The people talking or the people being talked about? The ones whose prosperity inspires such mean-spiritedness or the ones being mean? I thought so. Go forth and PROSPER. Prosper until you can't prosper any more and have an embarrassment of riches (and not just in the financial sense although that will come too). Be one of those people who fulfills his or her destiny and becomes what he or she is meant to be in every way. Have everything – a sound mind, a healthy body, great relationships, and financial freedom. Because? Because *that's* life lived abundantly and in Peace. And it's there for every single one of us.

91 - PEACE IN PEOPLE

❖

Have you ever been with a person who seems to know someone wherever he or she goes? And I'm not just talking about bumping into a friend at the market or on holiday when you both know you go there every year. I'm talking about knowing people in every country you visit, on every continent you've ever travelled to and in every town, village and city that you've ever had the pleasure of travelling through.

To some people that idea would fill them with dread, and yet to me that's something I aspire to. Why? Because I believe it's meant to be that way. I believe we are a global village and that in each part of this spectacular village, there are groups of people we could learn from. Wisdom we could use and filter into our own lives. Traditions we'd be wise to adopt and stories that could change our lives unrecognizably for the better.

Let me ask you a question: why shouldn't we know everyone else? Apart from the logistics of actually meeting the billions of people that inhabit our planet, I see no other reason. When I hear people say 'I have one or two close friends and a few acquaintances' I shudder. Why would you want so few people in your life? Think of what you're missing out on. Yes, there will be people that you would naturally want to spend more time with. And I still stand by my belief that if a person is truly toxic then I don't think any more time, if any, than is absolutely necessary should be spent in his or her company. But truly toxic people are actually few and far between. It's just that we give them far too much headspace and that means there's no room for anyone else. There's a whole planet of people out there and the more you fill your life with them the less time you'll have to think about what's lacking in your own life, as you'll be enriched by their presence. And, you'll soon come to realize there is absolutely nothing lacking in your life, because there is no 'lack', only the perception of it. And with that realization comes Peace.

92 - FU*K IT!

❖

Me: I've done all I can.

My Soul: I know. You've done well.

Me: I admit there are things I said and did that were not smart.

My Soul: Well, yes.

Me: But there was no malice, ever!

My Soul: I realize that.

Me: The intention was always pure. Always. I think I panicked.

My Soul: Yes, you probably did.

Me: I take full responsibility for my part.

My soul: Of course.

Me: My apology wasn't received well.

My Soul: It doesn't need to be. As long as your intention when apologizing was pure.

Me: It was.

My Soul: Cool. Only you'd know.

Me: It was too much for one person to handle. The whole thing was too much with all the other stuff going on.

My soul: Undoubtedly.

Me: I just thought I could manage it all.

My Soul: Of course you did.

Me: I need to move on now.

My soul: You do.

Me: Let it go.

My Soul: As soon as you feel you can. Do not hang on to this now. It serves no purpose to anybody.

Me: I can do no more, can I?

My Soul: I know you and I can safely say that you can do no more.

Me: Then Fuck it!

My Soul: Fuck it!

Me: … I feel better. Lighter.

My Soul: You feel more Peace-full. That's what you're experiencing.

Me: Yes, yes I am. Wow, wow, wow! I had no idea. I had no idea that this even existed. The lightness, the letting go, the Peace. I'm crying, I'm sorry, I don't know what to do. I'm so relieved.

My Soul: You're in Peace. Welcome.

93 - THE DIFFERENT JOURNEYS OF FAITH AND DOUBT

❖

What you believe in will determine where you go. What happens to you along the way and how you feel as you're treading the journey through life will determine where you go also. It is easy to take the path of no belief, more commonly known as doubt, that's for sure. But doubt will lead you only one way, down. How low will you allow doubt to take you before you employ FAITH, which will enable you to soar?

Doubt will ensure that the journey you take with it *appears* easy and true. But appearances can be deceptive. While faith will insist on courage which is a lot more work for you. But the investment will be worth it. Doubt will move speedily towards the bottom of the pile. Which is good if you like speed but not so good if you don't like being at the bottom of the pile! Faith will appear to travel so slowly that at times you'll feel as if you're in total darkness. And then, you'll spot a glimmer of light, which will grow and grow until the light overtakes the darkness. That's YOUR faith at work. Faith enlarges light.

It's entirely up to you what path you take but know this: both doubt and faith are only capable of moving in one direction. No matter what you do, you will not be able to alter the direction that these two travel in and they will not travel together. Choose. Choose to go up, towards Peace. It's great up here.

94 - FINDING PEACE WHEN YOUR DREAMS ARE ON HOLD

❖

The older you get, the more you rack up dreams that you haven't yet had come to pass. And if you stop and dwell on those dreams hanging there, unfulfilled, dreams that seemingly once contained so much hope and faith, it can be really hard not to feel frustrated and also ever-so-slightly heartbroken. I have no definitive answer for why some of our dreams don't happen in the way we want them. I have such dreams as well and this is how I deal with them:

Since I was a very young girl I have wanted to act – on the stage or on the screen, I didn't really care as I loved both mediums equally and it was all about the work itself for me. To be given a script and begin the journey of a character who had started life in the mind of another person and been written for an actor to portray is unlike any other thrill that I've experienced. As an actor, you get to live with that person for the duration of the production;

yet, when it all finishes, depending on the character or the production itself, you can often be left entirely bereft of the 'person' who was in your life for that time.

Acting was my dream. I felt deep in my heart that I was born to be an actor. That out of so many people who tried it, I would be one of that special group who would do it for the rest of my working life. I had graduated from one of the top drama schools in the world and was working professionally, when I found myself, one night after an industry-related party, in a particularly nasty situation that I wasn't able to cope with. I was left severely traumatized and truly believe that something died in me that night. I recently realized that since then I have subconsciously equated my dream of an acting career with that situation. It was impossible for me to go on with it after that night, so I stopped. I told all my friends that I wasn't doing it any more and I told my agent that I was no longer pursuing that path. It's a decision that I've also repeatedly beaten myself up about for many years now.

A very short time after that though, I met my husband, fell in love and have since built a life and a family with him, which continues to grow. But every now and again I get a flash of what life could have been like had I pursued the dream I had for so long. It doesn't come to mind as regret, as such, but I do wonder. About a year ago I felt that I couldn't sit around and wonder any longer and I made steps to try and pick up where I had left off. After a very positive start, the whole endeavour came to an abrupt end and it was totally clear to me that this wasn't going to be a path that I could pursue successfully at this time in my life. I felt relief and Peace when I let it go for a second time, but does that also mean that my love for it has disappeared? No. Goodness, no. To this very day, I still get caught up in wondering what it must be like to take on various projects or characters when I see something on TV or at the theatre that I particularly love. But I cannot live a life of regret or wishful thinking. So, I allow those feelings of wistfulness to flow through me. I don't resist them, and then I immediately find something in my life right now that makes me feel confidence or gratitude for what I have. And I sit with that until I know that any feelings of sadness have passed. I've come to realize that there is more than one way for me to add value to the world and so I pursue those things with vigour, such as writing for instance.

I don't know the end of my story, as I haven't lived to the end of my life just yet. And I no longer have to have hindsight in order for me to know that things will work out absolutely perfectly. I just have to find my Peace in any given situation. I have to find it, hold on to it and know that, whatever I am doing, if I am at Peace I am doing exactly the right thing for that moment.

95 - PEACE: SEE IT, THEN BE IT

❖

What does Peace look like to you? Can you see it in your imagination or is it more than you could ever hope for to have a life of Peace? Ah, well there's the rub, because the order of your faith has to change. You have to *see* Peace in your mind before it will translate into your life. So, let's say that you can see it in your mind's eye. What is it you see when you visualize Peace in your life? Is it a life with no conflict? If it is then SEE it, imagine it, dream it, feel it, BE it!

Is it a life with no health issues? If it is then SEE it, imagine it, dream it, feel it, BE it!

Is it a life with no money worries? If it is then SEE it, imagine it, dream it, feel it, BE it!

Is it a life with no anxiety? If it is then SEE it, imagine it, dream it, feel it, BE it!

SEE the change to BE the change.

96 - IMPOSSIBLE TO SHAME

❖

In times gone by, to shame people would mean that they would have to wear a large scarlet letter on their clothing or spend time in the stocks in the middle of the village. Not many people would know that they had been publicly shamed unless the news travelled outside of the village and on to the next one. Today, you can be globally shamed overnight via the internet – where not a few people are involved, but sometimes millions. How does a person recover from a shaming of that magnitude? It can be quite terrifying to have something, be it an image or writing, that is meant to shame you put online for all to see. I was shamed once. Wrongfully in a tabloid. And it took almost two years for me to pluck up the courage to act to get the article in question removed. Even so, I lost confidence, faith and became nervous.

How did I get through it? I healed myself through forgiveness (both of myself and others), meditation, love and through seeking Peace in all aspects of my life.

But what about those who do not know how to do that?

What about the children who are shamed? The men and women who do nothing wrong but simply come up against the wrong type of person? The person who has his or her career destroyed by someone who uses the internet as a weapon?

This is a process that we, as a race, are working through right now. It's all pretty new to us and we are all finding ways of coping with being a potential victim. But I have young children, so what am I doing to raise them in a way that the effects of 'shaming' will be minimal?

Some people retaliate by facing the 'haters' head on and standing up for themselves. And, in my opinion, this can really be the only way forward. I am going to raise my children to know that it is impossible for others to shame you unless you allow it. If you have your personal boundaries firmly in place then any attempts at shaming will simply bounce off of them like bullets off a mighty superhero shield. And in teaching them this philosophy I am learning more about it myself. Recently, I was put in the position of being threatened with a 'shaming' again! How did I react this time? Well, I came to the conclusion that I could no longer be shamed into not living my life the way it should be lived. Namely in Peace, Joy and Abundance. The choice has been made, the die cast and the 'takeaway' from this chapter is this – It is impossible to shame those who **will not** be shamed. I'm talking about people like you and me. Normal people who are open to all that life has for them and refuse to be stopped in their tracks. There is Peace in choosing to refuse to be shamed. It is a journey and it may be hard, but the journey ends in Peace.

97 - WHY NOT?

❖

The moment you answer the question: 'Will my dreams ever be fulfilled?' with the reply 'Why not?' is the moment the wheels will be put into motion to create them.

98 - THERE CAN BE PEACE IN NOT CARING

❖

For years, I found it extremely difficult not to care. I cared about what people thought, what they did, who they spoke to, whether they had fun, whether they were happy, whether they were unhappy. You name it; I cared about it. But that isn't true care at all – it's worry and fear dressed up as caring.

The freedom, and then the avalanche of Peace, came for me when I stopped caring about the things that were other people's choices. Realizing that it's their choice if they're happy, sad, doing something they love or loathe, thinking about things or people that drive them nuts. And it's not my responsibility. My responsibility is to care and maintain my own life, health, Peace and joy. My responsibility is to love and respect those around me. If someone is utterly toxic then I'm not taking care of myself by having him or her in my life as it makes it hard to sustain a life of Peace.

The fact is sometimes there's Peace in not caring, even though it might go against every caring bone in your body (it did mine). But if you can separate the authentic care that you will rightly have for another person from the 'care' that is actually fuelled by worry and fear, you'll have the ability to choose. Choose the path that leads to more Peace.

99 - THE PEACE IN LIGHTHEARTEDNESS

❖

We've covered so many 'heavy' topics in this book and the ways in which we can find our way back to Peace through them. But one of the most effective day-to-day methods of ensuring that you know deep Peace is when you have the ability to be lighthearted.

For a long time, I associated being lighthearted with not really making an effort and I could not have been more wrong. Being lighthearted about things means that you've made all the effort that is good for you and now you've let go. And it's in the letting go that there is Peace. Such profound Peace that it will knock your socks off and, and here's the absolute miracle in my case, you'll be able to banish your ego and stop taking yourself so seriously. Being lighthearted is not about not caring or being a doormat. It's not about letting the chips fall where they may. It's about knowing where to direct your attention. And believe me, there's very little other than Peace, Joy and Abundance that your attention should be on.

Explore lightheartedness. It'll feel strange at first, especially for us 'doers' out there. We'll feel as if we've lost a certain amount of control. Until you realize that the things you have let go of are not really worth being bothered about. Instead they have been replaced by things of such value and worth that you'll wonder why you kept them outside the room of your life for so long.

100 - BE THE ONE!

❖

Be the **one** who says: 'No, it will not be that way.'

Be the **one** who says: 'Yes, I will make sure this happens.'

Be the **one** who won't be driven from your path of Peace.

Be the **one** who loves first and then makes decisions.

Be the **one** who uses wisdom, instead of force.

Be the **one** who treats calmness as the miraculous salve that it is.

Be the **one** who lives in faith, instead of just wishing.

Be the **one** who has confidence, instead of conforms.

Be the **one** who believes and receives.

Be the **one** who lives in freedom because you've forgiven.

Be the **one** who is open to everyone and closed to no one.

Be the **one** who cannot see lack, no matter how hard you look, and can only see abundance.

Be the **one** with a life that overflows, instead of a life that is scraping the bottom.

Be the **one** who seeks Peace, finds Peace and lives Peace.

What would happen if we were all **THE ONE**?

Peace on earth, that's what.

101 - JUST ONE MORE THING FROM ME BEFORE YOU GO!

❖

You are extraordinarily loveable, just the way you are. In fact, we would like more of you. So please give it to us.

Thank you and best wishes,

Everybody in the Whole World.

Printed in Great Britain
by Amazon